25 cushions to knit

25 cushions to knit

FANTASTIC CUSHIONS FOR EVERY ROOM IN YOUR HOME

Debbie Abrahams

COLLINS & BROWN

First published in the United Kingdom in 2004
First published in paperback in 2009 by
Collins & Brown
10 Southcombe Street
London
W14 0RA

An imprint of Anova Books Company Ltd

Photography by Lucinda Symons and Matthew Dickens

ISBN 978-1-84340-509-2

A CIP catalogue for this book is available from the British
Library.

10 9 8 7 6 5 4 3 2 1

Reproduction by Rival Colour Ltd, UK
Printed and bound by Imago, Singapore

This book can be ordered direct from the publisher.
Contact the marketing department, but try your bookshop first.

www.anovabooks.com

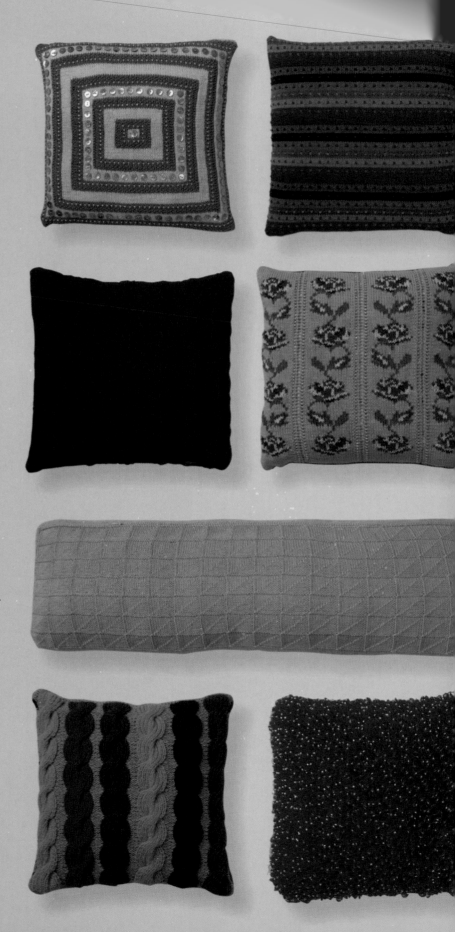

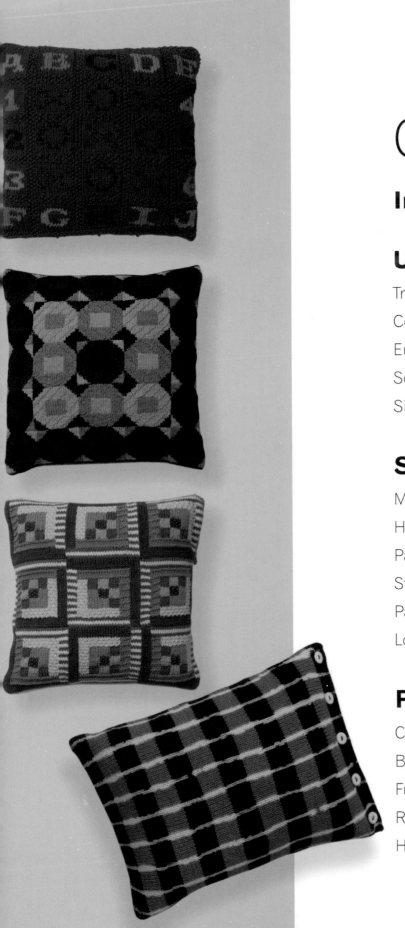

Contents

Our homes are important to us, and we all like to add personal touches to them to make them unique. In an age when there is a huge focus on interior design, it is becoming increasingly popular to make your own home furnishings. It is also an incredibly satisfying experience to handcraft something that will add style to your home and be enjoyed and admired by all who visit. This book gives you the opportunity to create well designed accessories for different rooms. All you need is a pair of knitting needles, some yarn, and a little patience! Cushions are easy to knit – there's no shaping to worry about – and you can experiment with new techniques like beading, cabling, or knitting with color, in a small achievable project. You can choose your own colorways as well so that your hand-knitted creations match your existing furnishings. There are 25 new designs and one old favorite to choose from in this book. They have been split into five different lifestyle settings to suit modern-day living. From the raw, fearless energy of Urban Cool to the restrained quiet of Modern Minimal, these cushions will add color, comfort, and warmth to your home. So what are you waiting for?!? Choose your lifestyle, choose your cushion, grab your needles, and get knitting!

Debbie Abrahams

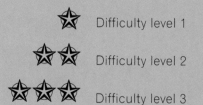

Difficulty level 1

Difficulty level 2

Difficulty level 3

These are a guide only. What some knitters find difficult, others find quite easy, so read the pattern before deciding whether or not to knit it.

Urban cool

Trash

Every season each new fashion story offers a reinvention of denim. Over the years we have seen it ripped, frayed, bleached, sand-blasted, over-dyed, embroidered, pre-creased, and stone-washed. It is a fabric long associated with work-wear, and for each new generation it continues to be a symbol of non-conformity. Trash invites you to experiment with the knitting equivalent of denim . Lines of bleach are dribbled across neat stripes and left until the color lifts, giving a rough, checkered effect. However, you can leave the bleach bottle in the bathroom cupboard and just enjoy the denim.

SIZE

12in × 16in (30cm × 40cm)

MATERIALS

1 pair US 6 (4mm/no.8) needles
1 pair US 5 (3.75mm/no.9) needles

Yarn

Rowan Denim
1¾oz (50g) balls

indigo (A)	2
light blue (B)	2
ecru (C)	1

Buttons

milk ceramic	5

Bleached version only
bleach
newspaper
sewing thread
needle
disposable gloves

GAUGE (TENSION)

Before washing
20 sts and 28 rows to 4in (10cm) measured over stockinette (stocking) stitch using US 6 (4 mm/no.8) needles.

ABBREVIATIONS

See page 127.

TECHNIQUES

Buttonholes, see page 123
Binding (casting) off buttonhole bands and buttonbands, see page 123
Darning in ends, see page 120.
Sewing up, see page 125.

KNIT

Front Panel

Both versions
Cast on 63 sts using US 6 (4mm/no.8) needles and yarn A.
20-row stripe patt repeat
ROW 1 (RS): Yarn A, knit.
ROW 2 (WS): Yarn A, purl.
ROWS 3–10: Rep rows 1–2 four times.
ROW 11: Yarn B, knit.
ROW 12: Yarn B, purl.
ROWS 13–20: Rep rows 11–12 four times.
Rep the 20-row patt repeat six times.
Buttonhole band
Change to US 5 (3.75mm/no.9) needles.
Rep patt repeat rows 1–4 once more. Cont in yarn A only.
NEXT ROW (RS) (BUTTONHOLE ROW): K4, [bind (cast) off 3 sts, K10 including st already on needle] four times, bind (cast) off 3 sts, K4 including st already on needle.
NEXT ROW (WS): P4, [turn work (RS facing), cast on 3 sts, turn work again (WS facing), P10] four times, turn work (RS facing), cast on 3 sts, turn work again (WS facing), P4.
Work a further 3 rows in stockinette (stocking) stitch, ending with a RS row.
With WS facing bind (cast) off sts.

Back Panel

Bleached version
Cast on 63 sts using US 6 (4mm/no.8) needles and yarn B.
**Working in stockinette (stocking) stitch throughout and beg with a RS row, rep the foll stripe sequence eight times in total.
15-row stripe patt repeat
Yarn B, 5 rows.
Yarn C, 5 rows.
Yarn A, 5 rows.
(120 rows)

Buttonband

Change to US 5 (3.75mm/no.9) needle. Yarn B only and cont in stockinette (stocking) stitch, work a further 10 rows.
NEXT ROW (RS): Purl (to form a fold-line for the buttonband).
NEXT ROW (WS): Purl.
Work a further 9 rows in stockinette (stocking) stitch, ending with a RS row.
Leave sts on needle.

Binding (casting) off the buttonband

With WS facing and using a US 5 (3.75mm/no.9) needle and yarn B, pick up all of the stitches across the knitting at the beginning of the buttonband, picking up the loops of yarn B. When the stitches are picked up the knitting needle should be parallel with the needle that is holding the stitches from the buttonband. Using a US 6 (4mm/no.8) needle bind (cast) off the stitches together.✳✳

Unbleached version

With RS facing using US 5 (3.75mm/no.9) needles and yarn C, pick up and knit 63 sts along the cast on edge of front panel.
NEXT ROW (WS): **Knit.**
Change to US 6 (4mm/no.8) needles.
Rep as for back panel (bleached version) from ✳✳ to ✳✳.

FINISHING

Bleached version

Before washing darn in ends on the WS of the work.

Using sewing thread, mark out the foll stitches in lines for bleaching by sewing a loose running stitch along them: stitches 4, 11, 18, 25, 32, 39, 46, 53, 60.

With RS facing upwards and the stripes vertical pin the front panel out flat onto a wad of newspaper.

Carefully dribble some bleach along each marked line. Do not to tilt the bottle too quickly to avoid flooding. If the lines wobble slightly don't worry—this will add to the look of the finished cushion.

It might be a good idea to try this out first on a scrap piece of knitting, such as your gauge (tension) sample, to get used to the flow of the bleach.

Remove the sewing thread. Leave for approx. 90 minutes (or until color has lifted sufficiently). If the bleach looks yellow in places, this should turn to white after the hot machine wash.

Thoroughly rinse the knitting several times in cold water.

Unbleached version

Darn in ends on the WS of the work.

Both versions

Wash panels in the washing machine on the hottest whites wash (70-90 degrees) with detergent. If possible, tumble-dry to near dryness to achieve maximum shrinkage.

Bleached version

Sew cast on edge of front panel to cast on edge of back panel.

Both versions

Sew side seams together (including the buttonhole band and buttonband at the top).
Sew buttons onto buttonband to correspond with buttonholes.

Cool cable

Soft, bulky cables in this all-over repeat design add a touch of comfort to the functional urban pad. The reverse stockinette (stocking) stitch background between the cables is knitted using a variegated yarn that gives it a slightly weathered look. This makes a great backdrop for the solid colored cables, which almost leap out at you from the knitting. The cables continue onto the back panels, but they are knitted completely in the solid colored yarn, creating a stark contrast to the front panel of this cushion cover.

SIZE

15in × 15in (38cm × 38cm)

MATERIALS

1 pair US 7 (4.5mm/no.7) needles
1 pair US 6 (4mm/no.8) needles
Cable needle

Colorway 1 (main picture)

Yarn

Rowan All Seasons Cotton
1¾oz (50g) balls
    purple (A)   5
Rowan All Seasons Cotton Printed
1¾oz (50g) balls
    purple/cream mix (B)   2

Buttons

    speckol ceramic   5

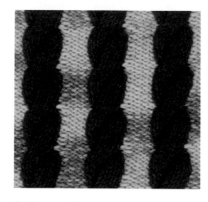

Colorway 2

Yarn

Rowan All Seasons Cotton
1¾oz (50g) balls
    charcoal (A)   5
Rowan All Seasons Cotton Printed
1¾oz (50g) balls
    gray/cream mix (B)   2

Buttons

    speckol ceramic   5

GAUGE (TENSION)

26 sts and 32 rows to 4in (10cm)
measured over cable patt using
US 7 (4.5mm/no.7) needles.

ABBREVIATIONS

c8b = cable 8 back: slip next
4 sts onto cable needle and hold
at back of work, K4, then K4 sts
from the cable needle
See also page 127.

TECHNIQUES

Cables, see page 122.
Buttonholes, see page 123.
Darning in ends, see page 120.
Blocking and pressing,
    see page 124.
Sewing up, see page 125.

KNIT

Front Panel

Cast on 100 sts using US 7
(4.5mm/no.7) needles in the foll
sequence:
[4B, 8A] eight times, 4B.
ROW 1 (RS): [P4B, K8A] eight
times, P4B.
ROW 2 (WS): [K4B, P8A] eight
times, K4B.
ROWS 3–6: Rep rows 1–2 twice
more
ROW 7: [P4B, c8b A] eight times,
P4B.
ROW 8: As row 2.

10-row patt repeat

ROW 1 (RS): [P4B, K8A] eight times, P4B.

ROW 2 (WS): [K4B, P8A] eight times, K4B.

ROWS 3–8: Rep rows 1–2 three times.

ROW 9: [P4B, c8b A] eight times, P4B.

ROW 10: As row 2.

Rep the 10-row patt repeat eleven times.

Rep patt repeat rows 1–2 once more.

Rep patt repeat row 1 once more, ending with a RS row.

(121 rows)

With WS facing bind (cast) off sts.

Buttonhole Panel

With RS facing pick up and knit 100 sts along bound (cast) off edge of front panel using US 7 (4.5mm/no.7) needles and yarn A only. (This pick up row is row 1 of the buttonhole panel.)

✻✻NEXT ROW (WS): [K4, P8] eight times, K4.

NEXT ROW (RS): [P4, K8] eight times, P4.

Rep the last 2 rows once more.

Rep the first row only once more.

10-row patt repeat

ROW 1 (RS): [P4, c8b] eight times, P4.

ROW 2 (WS): [K4, P8] eight times, K4.

ROW 3: [P4, K8] eight times, P4.

ROWS 4–9: Rep rows 2–3, three times more.

ROW 10: Rep row 2.

Rep the 10-row patt repeat five times in total.

Rep patt repeat row 1 once more.

(57 rows)

NEXT ROW (WS) (DEC): [K4, P2tog, P1, P2tog, P1, P2tog] eight times, K4.

(76 sts)✻✻

Buttonhole band

Change to US 6 (4mm/no.8) needles.

Work 2 rows in stockinette (stocking) stitch.

NEXT ROW (RS) (BUTTONHOLE ROW): K2, bind (cast) off next 2 sts, K15 including st already on needle, [bind (cast) off next 2 sts, K16 including st already on needle] twice, bind (cast) off next 2 sts, K15 including st already on needle, bind (cast) off next 2 sts, K2 including st already on needle.

NEXT ROW (WS): P2, turn work (RS facing), cast on 2 sts, turn work again (WS facing), P15, [turn work (RS facing), cast on 2 sts, turn work again, (WS facing) P16] twice, turn work (RS facing), cast on 2 sts, turn work again (WS facing), P15, turn work (RS facing), cast on 2 sts, turn work again (WS facing), P2.

NEXT ROW (RS): Knit.

With WS facing bind (cast) off sts knitwise.

Buttonband Panel

With RS facing pick up and knit 100 sts along cast on edge of front panel using US 7 (4.5mm/no.7) needles and yarn A only. (This pick up row is row 1 of the buttonband panel.)

Rep instructions for buttonhole panel from ✻✻ to ✻✻.

Buttonband

Using US 6 (4mm/no.8) needles and beg with a RS row, work 14 rows in stockinette (stocking) stitch.

Bind (cast) off sts.

FINISHING

Darn in ends on the WS of the work. With WS facing and using a damp pressing cloth and a cool iron, lightly press the cushion cover.

Mark the center point along side seam edges of front panel. Sew side seams of buttonhole panel to front panel, ensuring that buttonholes are in line with the marked center point.

Sew side seams of buttonband panel to front panel, inserting broad stockinette (stocking) stitch border at finished edge under the finished edge of the buttonhole panel, and sew down into place.

Turn cover inside out and carefully press seams.

Sew buttons onto buttonband to correspond with buttonholes.

Euphoria

There are some pieces of music that make the hairs stand up on the back of my neck—music that gives me goose-bumps all over. If that heightened sense of excitement triggered by such pieces of music could be translated into line and color, this would be it. The intensity of the colors and the proximity of the stripes to one another reflect the rising and falling emotions evoked by the music I love to listen to.

SIZE

12in × 16in (30cm × 40cm)

MATERIALS

1 pair US 2/3 (3mm/no.11) needles
1 pair US 2 (2.75mm/no.12) needles
1 US 2/3 (3mm/no.11) circular needle
   24in (60cm)

Colorway 1 (main picture front)

Yarn

Rowan Glace Cotton
1¾oz (50g) balls

palest pink (A)	1
purple (B)	1
orange (C)	1
pink (D)	1
lilac (E)	3
deep magenta (F)	1
white (G)	1

Buttons

orchid wine ceramic	5

Colorway 2 (main picture back)

Yarn

Rowan Glace Cotton
1¾oz (50g) balls

light beige (A)	1
bright blue (B)	1
orange (C)	1
pink (D)	1
aqua (E)	3
green (F)	1
cream (G)	1

Buttons

spur ceramic	5

GAUGE (TENSION)

25 sts and 34 rows to 4in (10cm) measured over stockinette (stocking) stitch using US 2/3 (3mm/no.11) needles.

ABBREVIATIONS

See page 127.

TECHNIQUES

Stripes using dp needles,
   see page 120.
Buttonholes, see page 123.
Darning in ends, see page 120.
Blocking and pressing,
   see page 124.
Sewing up, see page 125.

KNIT

Front Panel

Cast on 77 sts using US 2/3 (3mm/no.11) circular needle and yarn A.

47-row stripe patt repeat
Working in stockinette (stocking) stitch work stripe patt repeat as folls:

ROWS 1–5: **Yarn A.**
ROWS 6–8: **Yarn B.**
ROWS 9–12: **Yarn C.**
ROWS 13–18: **Yarn D.**
ROWS 19–20: **Yarn A.**
ROWS 21–23: **Yarn E.**
ROWS 24–27: **Yarn F.**
ROW 28: **Yarn D.**
ROWS 29–30: **Yarn G.**
ROWS 31–34: **Yarn D.**
ROWS 35–36: **Yarn E.**
ROW 37: **Yarn A.**
ROW 38: **Yarn E.**
ROWS 39–40: **Yarn B.**
ROW 41: **Yarn E.**
ROWS 42–43: **Yarn G.**
ROW 44: **Yarn E.**
ROWS 45–47: **Yarn D.**
Rep the 47-row patt repeat twice in total.
Rep rows 1–39 once more, ending with a RS row.
(133 rows)
Bind (cast) off sts.

Buttonhole Panel

With RS facing and using a US 2 (2.75mm/no.12) needle and yarn F (colorway 1) or yarn C (colorway 2), pick up and knit 77 sts along the bound (cast) off edge of the front panel.
✶✶NEXT ROW (WS): Knit.
Slip sts back onto left-hand needle so that the WS is facing you again.
Using yarn E, purl 1 row.
Change to US 2/3 (3mm/no.11) circular needle.

20-row patt repeat using yarn E only
ROW 1 (RS): [K7, (P1, K1) three times, P1] five times, K7.
ROW 2 (WS): P8, [(K1, P1) twice, K1, P9] four times, [K1, P1] twice, K1, P8.
ROWS 3–10: Rep rows 1–2 four times.
ROW 11: [(P1, K1) three times, P1, K7] five times, [P1, K1] three times, P1.
ROW 12: [P1, K1] three times, [P9, (K1, P1) twice, K1] four times, P9, [K1, P1] three times.
ROW 13–20: Rep rows 11–12 four times.
Rep the 20-row patt repeat twice in total.
Rep rows 1–19 once more, ending with a RS row.
(59 rows)
Buttonhole Band
Change to US 2 (2.75mm/no.12) needles.
NEXT ROW (WS): Using yarn E, knit.
Knit a further 2 rows (this forms a purl ridge).
NEXT ROW (RS): K4, [P3, K3] twelve times, K1.
NEXT ROW (WS): P4, [K3, P3] twelve times, P1.
Rep the last 2 rows once more✶✶.

NEXT ROW (RS) (BUTTONHOLE ROW): K4, P3, [bind (cast) off next 3 sts, P3 including st already on needle, K3, P3, K3, bind (cast) off next 3 sts, K3 including st already on needle, P3, K3, P3] twice, bind (cast) off next 3 sts, P3 including st already on needle, K4.

NEXT ROW (WS): P4, K3 [turn work (RS facing), cast on 3 sts, turn work again (WS facing), K3, P3, K3, P3, turn work (RS facing), cast on 3 sts, turn work again (WS facing), P3, K3, P3, K3] twice, turn work (RS facing), cast on 3 sts, turn work again (WS facing), K3, P4.

NEXT ROW (RS): K4, [P3, K3] twelve times, K1.

NEXT ROW (WS): P4, [K3, P3] twelve times, P1.

NEXT ROW (RS): Using yarn F (colorway 1) or yarn C (colorway 2), work 1 more row keeping sts as set in rib patt.

With WS facing, bind (cast) off sts knitwise.

Buttonband Panel

With RS facing and using a US 2 (2.75mm/no.12) needle and yarn F (colorway 1) or yarn C (colorway 2), pick up and knit 77 sts along the cast on edge of the front panel.

Rep instructions for buttonhole panel from ✳✳ to ✳✳.

Buttonband

Keeping sts correct, work a further 14 rows in rib patt.

With RS facing, bind (cast) off sts.

FINISHING

Darn in ends on the WS of the work. With WS facing and using a damp pressing cloth and a moderate iron, lightly press the cushion cover.

Mark the center point along side seam edges of front panel.

Sew side seams of buttonhole panel to front panel ensuring that buttonholes are in line with the marked center point.

Sew side seams of buttonband panel to front panel, inserting the broad rib stitch border at finished edge under the finished edge of buttonhole panel, and sew down into place.

Turn cover inside out and press seams.

Sew buttons onto buttonband, to correspond with buttonholes.

Scruff

This fun and funky design uses loop stitch to give a fake fur effect. The soft mohair loops in vibrant shades are threaded with twinkling glass beads to add extra sparkle. This creates a fluffy, tactile fabric that begs to be picked up and stroked. You could experiment with multi-colored loops for a really wild effect, or put together your own color combinations to match your furnishings.

SIZE
14in × 14in (35cm × 35cm)

MATERIALS
1 pair US 5 (3.75mm/no.9) needles
1 pair US 3 (3.25mm/no.10) needles

Colorway 1 (main picture)
Yarn
Rowan Wool Cotton
1¾oz (50g) balls
   aqua (A)   3
Rowan Kidsilk Haze
1¾oz (25g) balls
Note: This yarn is used triple throughout.
   bright pink (B)   3

Beads
⅛in (3mm) pebble beads
   silver   1000 approx.
   turquoise   1000 approx.

Buttons
   simply red ceramic   5

Colorway 2
Yarn
Rowan Wool Cotton
1¾oz (50g) balls
   cream (A)   3
Rowan Kidsilk Haze
1¾oz (25g) balls
Note: This yarn is used triple throughout.
   white (B)   3

Beads
⅛in (3mm) pebble beads
   silver   2000 approx.

Buttons
   milk ceramic   5

Colorway 3
Yarn
Rowan Wool Cotton
1¾oz (50g) balls
   yellow (A)   3
Rowan Kidsilk Haze
1¾oz (25g) balls
Note: This yarn is used triple throughout.
   pale blue (B)   3

Beads
⅛in (3mm) pebble beads
   silver   1000 approx.
   pearl   1000 approx.

Buttons
   simply blue ceramic   5

Colorway 4
Yarn
Rowan Wool Cotton
1¾oz (50g) balls
   orange (A)   3
Rowan Kidsilk Haze
1¾oz (25g) balls
Note: This yarn is used triple throughout.
   green (B)   3

Beads
⅛in (3mm) pebble beads
   red   2000 approx.

Buttons
   simply green ceramic   5

GAUGE (TENSION)
23 sts and 30 rows to 4in (10cm) measured over loop stitch patt using US 5 (3.75mm/no.9) needles.

ABBREVIATIONS

ml = (make loop): K next st leaving st on left needle, bring yarn forward between needles, slide a bead up so that it is sitting about ¾in (2cm) away from the needle, and wrap the yarn with bead round thumb of left-hand to make a loop, take yarn between needles to back of work and K same st again, slipping st off left needle. Bring yarn forward between needles and back over needle to WS of work. Lift the 2 sts just made over this loop.
See also page 127.

TECHNIQUES

Loop stitch, see page 121.
Buttonholes, see page 123.
Darning in ends, see page 120.
Blocking and pressing,
   see page 124.
Sewing up, see page 125.

KNIT
Front Panel

Cast on 80 sts using US 5 (3.75mm/no.9) needles and yarn A.

Colorway 1
Thread alternate silver and turquoise beads onto yarn B.

Colorway 2
Thread silver beads onto yarn B.

Colorway 3
Thread alternate silver and pearl beads onto yarn B.

Colorway 4
Thread red beads onto yarn B.

All colorways
4-row patt repeat
ROW 1 (WS): Yarn A, knit.
ROW 2 (RS): [K1A, using yarn B, ml], rep until 2 sts rem, K2A.
ROW 3: Yarn A, knit.

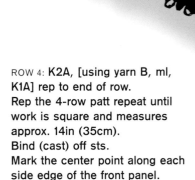

ROW 4: K2A, [using yarn B, ml, K1A] rep to end of row.
Rep the 4-row patt repeat until work is square and measures approx. 14in (35cm).
Bind (cast) off sts.
Mark the center point along each side edge of the front panel.

Buttonhole Panel

With RS facing pick up and knit 80 sts along bound (cast) off edge of front panel using US 3 (3.25mm/no.10) needles and yarn A only.
**NEXT ROW (WS): Knit.
Change to US 5 (3.75mm/no.9) needles.
NEXT ROW (RS): K40, m1, K40. (81 sts)
NEXT ROW (WS): Purl.
Beg with a RS row work in stockinette (stocking) stitch until panel is 5 rows shorter than marked center point on front panel, ending with a WS row.**

Buttonhole band
Change to US 3 (3.25mm/no.10) needles.
Beg with a RS row work 4 more rows in stockinette (stocking) stitch.
NEXT ROW (RS) (BUTTONHOLE ROW): K5, [bind (cast) off next 3 sts, K14 including st already on needle] four times, bind (cast) off next 3 sts, K5 including st already on needle.
NEXT ROW (WS): P5, [turn work (RS facing), cast on 3 sts, turn work again (WS facing), P14] four times, turn work (RS facing), cast on 3 sts, turn work again (WS facing), P5.
Work a further 8 rows in stockinette (stocking) stitch.
With RS facing bind (cast) off sts knitwise.

Buttonband Panel

With RS facing pick up and knit 80 sts along cast on edge of front panel using US 3 (3.25mm/no.10) needles and yarn A only.
Rep instructions for buttonhole panel from ** to **.
Buttonband
Change to US 3 (3.25mm/no.10) needles.
Beg with a RS row work a further 16 rows in stockinette (stocking) stitch.
Bind (cast) off sts.

FINISHING

Darn in ends on the WS of the work. With WS facing and using a moderate iron and a damp pressing cloth PRESS BACK PANELS ONLY.
   Sew side seams of buttonhole panel to front panel ensuring that buttonholes are in line with the marked center point.
   Sew side seams of buttonband panel to front panel, inserting broad stockinette (stocking) stitch border at finished edge under the finished edge of the buttonhole panel, and sew down into place.
   Sew buttons onto buttonband to correspond with buttonholes.

Sixties circles

Popular household artifacts from the 1960s have been reinvented by today's designers to create contemporary accessories for the home. This design is inspired by a personal favorite of mine—those shimmering curtains made from small colored discs of plastic that were popular in the 1960s and are making a comeback now. The neat arrangement of the circles and the bright semi-transparent colors in these curtains are interpreted in an all-over intarsia design that is repeated on both front and back panels.

SIZE

16in × 16in (40cm × 40cm)

MATERIALS

1 pair US 5 (3.75mm/no.9) needles
1 pair US 3 (3.25mm/no.10) needles

Colorway 1 (main picture)

Yarn
Rowan Wool Cotton
1¾oz (50g) balls

purple (A)	3
green (B)	1
orange (C)	1
aqua (D)	1
soft yellow (E)	1

Buttons

simply orange ceramic	2
simply blue ceramic	2
simply green ceramic	1

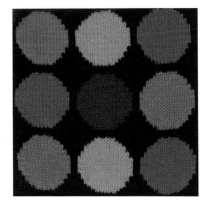

Colorway 2

Yarn
Rowan Wool Cotton
1¾oz (50g) balls

pink (A)	3
aqua (B)	1
purple (C)	1
green (D)	1
soft yellow (E)	1

Buttons

simply purple ceramic	2
simply blue ceramic	2
simply green ceramic	1

GAUGE (TENSION)

24 sts and 32 rows to 4in (10cm) measured over intarsia patt using US 5 (3.75mm/no.9) needles.

ABBREVIATIONS

See page 127.

TECHNIQUES

Intarsia knitting, see page 119.
Buttonholes, see page 123.
Binding (casting) off buttonhole bands and buttonbands, see page 123.
Blocking and pressing, see page 124.
Sewing up, see page 125.

KNIT

Front Panel

Cast on 96 sts using US 5 (3.75mm/no.9) needles and yarn A. Beg with a RS row, work until chart row 123 completed, ending with a RS row.

Buttonhole band
Change to US 3 (3.25mm/no.10) needles.
NEXT ROW (WS) (DEC ROW): Yarn A, P47, P2tog, P47.
(95 sts)
Beg with a RS row and yarn A, work 4 rows in stockinette (stocking) stitch.
NEXT ROW (RS) (BUTTONHOLE ROW): K6, [bind (cast) off next 3 sts, K17 including st already on needle] four times, bind (cast) off next 3 sts, K6 including st already on needle.
NEXT ROW (WS): P6, [turn work (RS facing), cast on 3 sts, turn work again (WS facing), P17] four times, turn work (RS facing), cast

on 3 sts, turn work again (WS facing), P6.
Cont in yarn A, work 4 rows in stockinette (stocking) stitch.
NEXT ROW (RS): Yarn B, knit.
NEXT ROW (WS): Yarn B, knit (this forms a fold line at the top of the buttonhole band).
Beg with a RS row work 5 rows in stockinette (stocking) stitch using yarn B.
NEXT ROW (WS) (BUTTONHOLE ROW): P6, [bind (cast) off next 3 sts, P17 including st already on needle] four times, bind (cast) off next 3 sts, P6 including st already on needle.
NEXT ROW (RS): K6, [turn work (WS facing), cast on 3 sts, turn work again (RS facing), K17] four times, turn work (WS facing), cast on 3 sts, turn work again (RS facing), K6.
Cont in yarn B, work 4 rows in stockinette (stocking) stitch, ending with a RS row.
Leave sts on needle.
With colored thread, mark row 124 of the front panel (the first row after the chart).

Key

■ purple (A)   □ K on RS, P on WS

■ green (B)

■ orange (C)

■ aqua (D)

□ soft yellow (E)

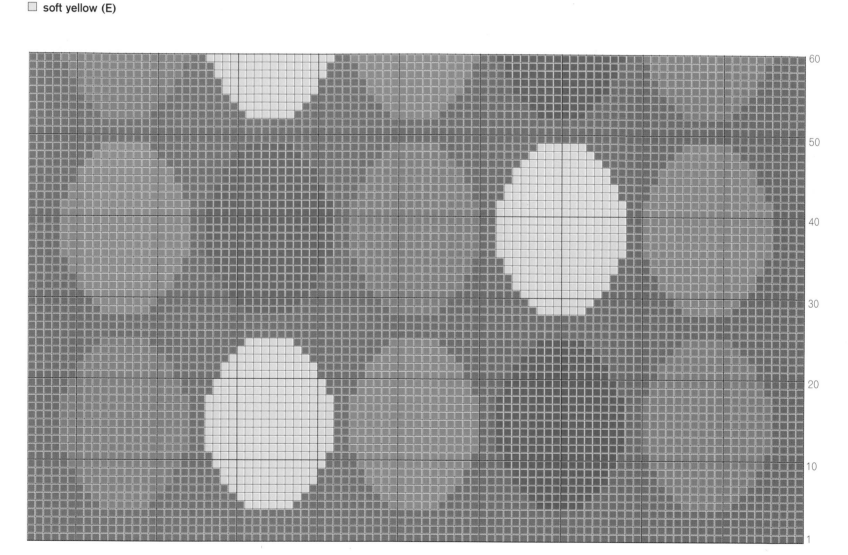

START OF SIXTIES CIRCLES CHART

■ purple (A)   ☐ K on RS, P on WS

■ green (B)

■ orange (C)

■ aqua (D)

☐ soft yellow (E)

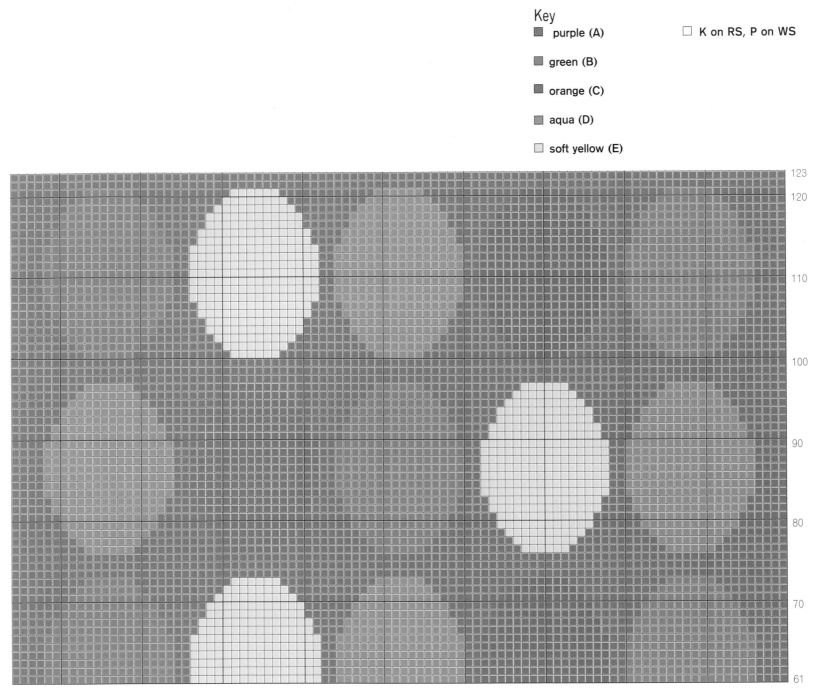

SIXTIES CIRCLES CHART CONTINUED

Back Panel

With RS facing and using US 3 (3.25mm/no.10) needles and yarn B pick up and knit 96 sts along the cast on edge of the front panel.

NEXT ROW: Knit.

Beg with a RS row, work until chart row 123 completed, ending with a RS row.

Buttonband

Change to US 3 (3.25mm/no.10) needles.

Beg with a RS row and yarn A only, work 11 rows in stockinette (stocking) stitch.

NEXT ROW (WS): Knit (to form a fold line at the top of the buttonband).

Work 11 rows in stockinette (stocking) stitch ending with a RS row.

Leave sts on needle.

With colored thread, mark row 124 of the back panel (the first row after the graph).

Both Panels

Binding (casting) off buttonhole band and buttonband

With WS facing and using a US 3 (3.25mm/no.10) needle and yarn A pick up all of the stitches across the WS of the knitting at the marked row 124 of the work. When the stitches are picked up the knitting needle should be parallel with the needle that is holding the stitches from the band. Using a US 5 (3.75mm/no.9) needle bind (cast) off the stitches together.

FINISHING

Darn in ends on the WS of the work. With WS facing and using a damp pressing cloth and a moderate iron, lightly press the cushion cover.

Sew side seams together (including the buttonhole band and buttonband at the top).

Sew buttons onto buttonband to correspond with buttonholes.

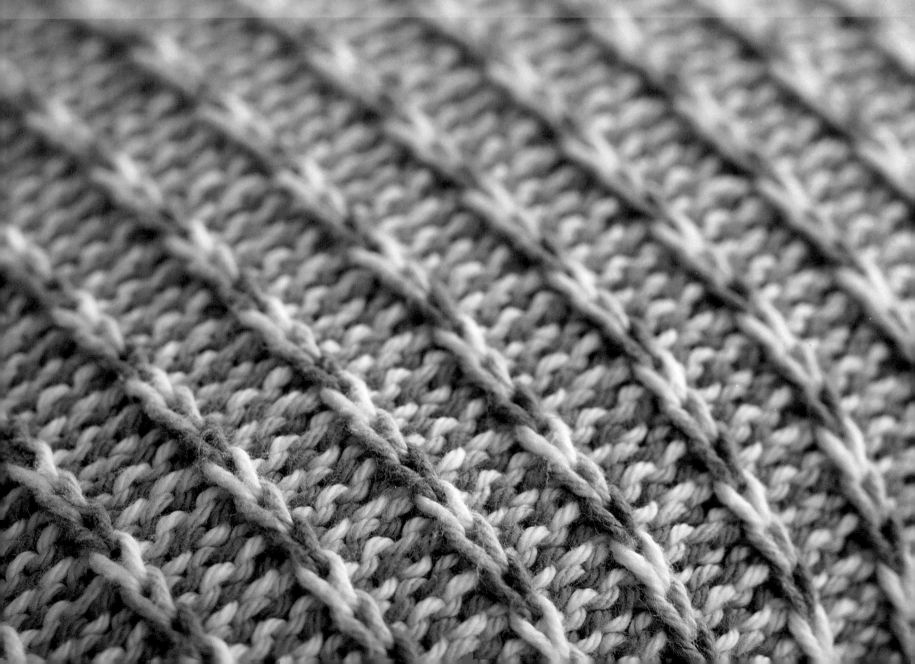

Shaker style

Milk jug stripe

The hugely collectable blue and white striped Cornish milk jug provided the inspiration for this crisp and simple design. It has been knitted in a mercerized cotton which creates a very flat and even fabric, simulating the smooth, glossy surface of the jug. A fastening of five plain white buttons across the top of the cushion cover complete this quick and easy to knit project.

SIZE
16in × 16in (40cm × 40cm)

MATERIALS
1 pair US 2/3 (3mm/no.11) needles
1 pair US 2 (2.75mm/no.12) needles
1 US 2/3 (3mm/no.11) circular needle
    24in (60cm)

Yarn
Rowan Glace Cotton
1¾oz (50g) balls
white (A)	4
mid blue (B)	2

Buttons
milk ceramic	5

GAUGE (TENSION)
25 sts and 34 rows to 4in (10cm) measured over stockinette stitch using US 2/3 (3mm/no.11) needles.

ABBREVIATIONS
See page 127.

TECHNIQUES
Stripes using dp needles,
    see page 120.
Buttonholes, see page 123.
Binding (casting) off buttonhole
    bands and buttonbands,
    see page 123.
Darning in ends, see page 120.
Blocking and pressing,
    see page 124.
Sewing up, see page 125.

KNIT
Front Panel
Cast on 101 sts using US 2/3 (3mm/no.11) circular needle and yarn A.
11-row stripe patt repeat
Working in stockinette (stocking) stitch work stripe patt repeat as folls:
Yarn A, 5 rows
Yarn B, 6 rows
Rep the 11-row patt repeat eleven times.
Work a further 6 rows using yarn A.
(127 rows)
Buttonhole band
Change to US 2 (2.75mm/no.12) needles)
Beg with a WS row and using yarn B, work 5 rows in stockinette (stocking) stitch.
NEXT ROW (RS) (BUTTONHOLE ROW):
Yarn B, K5, [bind (cast) off 3 sts, K19 including st already on needle] four times, bind (cast) off 3 sts, K5.

NEXT ROW (WS): Yarn B, P5, [turn work (RS facing), cast on 3 sts, turn work again (WS facing), P19] four times, turn work (RS facing), cast on 3 sts, turn work again (WS facing), P5.
Work a further 4 rows in stockinette (stocking) stitch using yarn B, ending with a WS row.
NEXT ROW (RS): Yarn A, knit.
NEXT ROW (WS): Yarn A, knit (to form a fold line for the buttonhole band). Yarn A, work 5 rows in stockinette (stocking) stitch.

NEXT ROW (WS) (BUTTONHOLE ROW):
Using yarn A: P5, [bind (cast) off 3 sts, P19] four times, bind (cast) off 3 sts, P5.
NEXT ROW (RS): Yarn A, K5, [turn work (RS facing), cast on 3 sts, turn work again (WS facing), K19] four times, turn work (RS facing), cast on 3 sts, turn work again (WS facing), K5.
Work a further 4 rows in stockinette (stocking) stitch using yarn A, ending with a RS row.
Leave sts on needle.

Back Panel

With RS facing and using a US 2 (2.75mm/no.12) needle and yarn B, pick up and knit 101 sts along the cast on edge of the front panel.

NEXT ROW (WS): Knit.

Change to US 2/3 (3mm/no.11) needles and yarn A.

10-row purl stitch patt repeat

ROW 1 (RS): Knit.

ROW 2 (WS): Purl.

ROWS 3–4: Rep rows 1–2.

ROW 5: K2, [P1, K3] twenty-four times, P1, K2.

ROW 6: Purl.

ROW 7: Knit.

ROWS 8–9: Rep rows 6–7.

ROW 10: P4, [K1, P3] twenty-four times, P1.

Rep the 10-row purl stitch patt repeat twelve times in total.

Rep rows 1–7 once more.

(127 rows)

Buttonband

Change to US 2 (2.75mm/no.12) needles).

Beg with a WS row and using yarn B, work 11 rows in stockinette (stocking) stitch.

NEXT ROW (RS): Yarn A, knit.

NEXT ROW (WS): Yarn A, knit (to form a fold line for the buttonband).

Yarn A, work 11 rows in stockinette (stocking) stitch ending with a RS row.

Leave sts on needle.

Both Panels

Binding (casting) off the buttonhole band and buttonband

With WS facing and using a US 2 (2.75mm/no.12) needle and yarn B, pick up all of the stitches across the WS of the knitting at the beginning of the band, picking up the loops of yarn B. When the stitches are picked up the knitting needle should be parallel with the needle that is holding the stitches from the band. Using a US 2/3 (3mm/no.11) needle bind (cast) off the stitches together.

FINISHING

Darn in ends on the WS of the work. With WS facing and using a damp pressing cloth and a moderate iron, lightly press the cushion cover.

Sew side seams together (including the buttonhole band and buttonband at the top).

Sew buttons to buttonband to correspond with buttonholes.

Hessian

Hessian is a hard-wearing woven fabric that has many practical and craft uses. For centuries it has been used on farms for sacking to store animal feed and hay, but in more recent years needle-workers have used it as the canvas for their intricate stitchwork. I have combined slipped and reverse stitches in a three-row stripe pattern repeat to create a knitted interpretation of this traditional woven fabric.

SIZE
16in × 16in (40cm × 40cm)

MATERIALS
1 pair US 5 (3.75mm/no.9) needles
1 pair US 2/3 (3mm/no.11) needles

Colorway 1 (main picture)
Yarn
Rowan Handknit DK Cotton
1¾oz (50g) balls

cream (A)	2
light beige (B)	3
brown (C)	3

Buttons
speckol ceramic	6

Colorway 2
Yarn
Rowan Handknit DK Cotton
1¾oz (50g) balls

cream (A)	2
pale gray (B)	3
mid blue (C)	3

Buttons
speckol ceramic	6

GAUGE (TENSION)
25 sts and 32 rows to 4in (10cm) measured over slip-stitch patt using US 5 (3.75mm/no.9) needles.

ABBREVIATIONS
See page 127.

TECHNIQUES
Buttonholes, see page 123.
Sewing up, see page 125.

KNIT
Front Panel
Cast on 101 sts using US 5 (3.75mm/no.9) needles and yarn A.
2-row slip-stitch patt repeat:
ROW 1 (RS): **P2, [yb, sl1 purlwise, yf, P3] twenty-four times, yb, sl1 purlwise, yf, P2.**
ROW 2 (WS): **K2, [P1, K3] twenty-four times, P1, K2.**

Beg with a RS row rep the 2-row patt repeat until the work is square, keeping in the foll color sequence throughout:
Yarn B, 1 row.
Yarn C, 1 row.
Yarn A, 1 row.
Bind (cast) off sts.
Mark the center point along the side seams of the front panel.

Buttonhole Panel

With RS facing pick up and knit 101 sts along bound (cast) off edge of front panel using US 2/3 (3mm/no.11) needles and yarn A.

NEXT ROW (WS): **Knit.**

✱✱Slip sts back onto left-hand needle so that the WS is facing you again.

Change to US 5 (3.75mm/no.9) needles.

Using yarn B only, purl 1 row.

2-row slip and seed (moss) stitch patt repeat

ROW 1 (RS): **P2, [yb, sl1 purlwise, yf, P3, K1, P3] twelve times, yb, sl1 purlwise, yf, P2.**

ROW 2 (WS): **[K2, P1, K2, P1, K1, P1] twelve times, K2, P1, K2.**

Rep the 2-row slip and seed (moss) stitch patt repeat until work is 4 rows shorter than the marked center point of the front panel, ending with a RS row.✱✱

Buttonhole band

Change to US 2/3 (3mm/no.11) needles and yarn C.

Beg with a WS row work a further 4 rows in slip and seed (moss) stitch patt repeat.

NEXT ROW (WS) (BUTTONHOLE ROW): **K2, P1, K1, bind (cast) off next 3 sts, P1 (this is the st already on the needle), K2, P1, K2, P1, K1, P1, K2, P1, K2, P1, bind (cast) off next 3 sts, K1 (this is the st already on the needle), P1, K2, P1, K1, P1, K2, P1, K2, P1, K1, P1, bind (cast) off next 3 sts, K2 (including st already on the needle), P1, K1, P1, K2, P1, K2, P1, K1, P1, K2, bind (cast) off next 3 sts, P1 (this is the st already on the needle), K1, P1, K2, P1, K2, P1, K1, P1, K2, P1, K1, bind (cast) off next 3 sts, P1 (this is the st already on the needle), K2, P1, K2, P1, K1, P1, K2, P1, K2, P1, bind (cast) off next 3 sts, K1 (this is the st already on the needle), P1, K2.**

NEXT ROW (RS): **P2, yb, sl1 purlwise, yf, P1, turn work (WS facing), cast on 3 sts, turn work again (RS facing), P3, yb, sl1 purlwise, yf, P3, K1, P3, yb, sl1 purlwise, yf, P3, turn work (WS facing), cast on 3 sts, turn work again (RS facing), P1, yb, sl1 purlwise, yf, P3, K1, P3, yb, sl1 purlwise, yf, P3, K1, P1, turn work (WS facing), cast on 3 sts, turn work again (RS facing), P3, K1, P3, yb, sl1 purlwise, yf, P3, K1, P3, turn work (WS facing), cast on 3 sts, turn work again**

(RS facing), P1, K1, P3, yb, sl1 purlwise, yf, P3, K1, P3, yb, sl1 purlwise, yf, P1, turn work (WS facing), cast on 3 sts, turn work again (RS facing), P3, yb, sl1 purlwise, yf, P3, K1, P3, yb, sl1 purlwise, yf, P3, turn work (WS facing), cast on 3 sts, turn work again (RS facing), P1, yb, sl1 purlwise, yf, P2.

Beg with a WS row and cont to use yarn C, work a further 2 rows in slip and seed (moss) stitch patt repeat. With WS facing bind (cast) off sts knitwise.

Buttonband Panel

With RS facing pick up and knit 101 sts along cast on edge of front panel using US 2/3 (3mm/no.11) needles and yarn A.

NEXT ROW (WS): **Knit.**

Using yarn C, rep patt instructions for buttonhole panel from ✱✱ to ✱✱.

Buttonband

Change to US 2/3 (3mm/no.11) needles.

Beg with a WS row and cont to use yarn C, work a further 14 rows in slip and seed (moss) stitch patt repeat.

Bind (cast) off sts.

FINISHING

Sew side seams of buttonhole panel to front panel ensuring that buttonholes are in line with the marked center point.

Sew side seams of buttonband panel to front panel, inserting broad slip and seed (moss) stitch border at finished edge under the finished edge of the buttonhole panel, and sew down into place.

Turn cover inside out and press seams.

Sew buttons onto buttonband to correspond with buttonholes.

Patchwork hearts

Here, the ever-popular heart motif is combined with denim to create a cushion cover that has a welcoming appeal. The heart motif is widely used in patchwork and is associated with the comforts of home. The front panel uses two different shades of denim yarn to create a checkerboard pattern. The back panel is knitted in a striped basket-weave stitch with reverse stitches to give the effect of rows of hand-stitching.

SIZE

16in × 16in (40cm × 40cm)

MATERIALS

1 pair US 6 (4mm/no.8) needles
1 pair US 3 (3.25mm/no.10) needles

Yarn

Rowan Denim
1¾oz (50g) balls
light blue (A)   4
indigo (B)   4
Rowan Handknit DK Cotton
1¾oz (50g) balls
red (C)   small amount

Beads

⅛in (4mm) pebble beads
red   432
pearl   243

Buttons

milk ceramic   6

GAUGE (TENSION)

Before washing
20 sts and 28 rows to 4in (10cm)
measured over stockinette
(stocking) stitch using US 6
(4mm/no.8) needles.

ABBREVIATIONS

pb = place bead: thread beads
onto yarn before starting to knit
each section:
(RS): with yarn forward, slide bead
up yarn, slip 1 stitch purlwise, yarn
back leaving bead in front of the
slipped stitch.
(WS): with yarn back, slide bead
up yarn, slip 1 stitch purlwise, yarn
forward leaving bead in front of
slipped stitch.
See also page 127.

TECHNIQUES

Intarsia knitting, see page 119.
Knitting with beads, see page 120.
Buttonholes, see page 123.
Sewing up, see page 125.

KNIT
Front Panel

Cast on 93 sts using US 6
(4mm/no.8) needles, in the foll
sequence:
Yarn A, 14 sts.
Yarn B, 13 sts.
Yarn A, 13 sts.
Yarn B, 13 sts.
Yarn A, 13 sts.
Yarn B, 13 sts.
Yarn A, 14 sts.
Beg with a RS row, continue to
work from chart repeating the 26-
st patt repeat twice within each
row and the 46-row patt repeat
three times.
Rep chart rows 1–22 once again.
(160 rows)
With RS facing and using yarn B,
bind (cast) off sts.

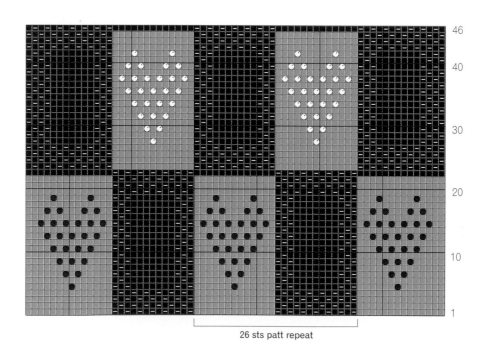

26 sts patt repeat

PATCHWORK HEARTS CHART

Key

■ light blue (A)

■ indigo (B)

● red bead

◔ pearl bead

□ K on RS, P on WS

⊟ P on RS, K on WS

Buttonhole Panel

With RS facing pick up and knit 93 sts along bound (cast) off edge of front panel using US 3 (3.25mm/no.10) needles and yarn C.

✳✳NEXT ROW (WS): Knit.
Break off yarn C.
Change to US 6 (4mm/no.8) needles and yarn A.
NEXT ROW (RS): Knit.
NEXT ROW (WS): P8A, [K7A, P7A] six times, P1A.
NEXT ROW (RS): K8A, [P7A, K7A] six times, K1A.
NEXT ROW (WS): P8A, [K7A, P7A] six times, P1A.

12-row patt repeat
ROW 1 (RS): P8B, [K7B, P7B] six times, P1B.
ROW 2 (WS): K8B, [P7B, K7B] six times, K1B.
ROWS 3–6: Rep rows 1–2 twice.
ROW 7: K8A, [P7A, K7A] six times, K1A.
ROW 8: P8A, [K7A, P7A] six times, P1A.
ROWS 9–12: Rep rows 7–8 twice.
Rep the 12-row patt repeat six times in total.**✳✳**

Buttonhole band
Worked in yarn B only.
Change to US 3 (3.25mm/no.10) needles.
NEXT ROW (RS): [K1, P1] to last st, K1.
Rep the last row three times more.
NEXT ROW (RS) (BUTTONHOLE ROW): [K1, P1] twice, K1, [cast off next 3 sts, (K1, P1) six times including st already on needle, K1] five times, bind (cast) off next 3 sts, [K1, P1] twice including st already on needle, K1.
NEXT ROW (WS): [K1, P1] twice, K1, [turn work (RS facing), cast on 3 sts, turn work again (WS facing), (K1, P1) six times, K1] five times, turn work (RS facing), cast on 3 sts, turn work again (WS facing), [K1, P1] twice, K1.
Keeping seed (moss) stitch patt

correct work a further 3 rows, ending with a RS row. With WS facing bind (cast) off sts knitwise.

Buttonband Panel

With RS facing pick up and knit 93 sts along the cast on edge of front panel using US 3 (3.25mm/no.10) needles and yarn C. Rep instructions for buttonhole panel from ✳✳ to ✳✳.

Buttonband
Yarn B only.
Using US 3 (3.25mm/no.10) needles and beginning with a RS row, work 18 rows in seed (moss) stitch as folls: [K1, P1] to last st. K1, on every row.
Bind (cast) off sts knitwise.

FINISHING

Darn in ends on the WS of the work.

Place the cushion cover inside a protective wash-bag and machine wash on the hottest whites wash (70–90 degrees) with detergent.

If possible, tumble-dry to near dryness to achieve maximum shrinkage.

Mark the center point along side seam edges of front panel.

Sew side seams of buttonhole panel to front panel ensuring that buttonholes are in line with the marked center point.

Sew side seams of buttonband panel to front panel, inserting broad seed (moss) stitch border at finished edge under the finished edge of the buttonhole panel, and sew down into place.

Turn cover inside out and press seams.

Sew buttons onto buttonband to correspond with buttonholes.

Stars and stripes

In this design, reverse stockinette (stocking) stitch stripes and textured and outlined stars are worked in a mixture of vibrant colors to give these familiar symbols a refreshing new twist. The front panel is knitted in three separate strips that are then sewn together to form one block, making this small cushion a quick and easy project to knit.

SIZE

12in × 12in (30cm × 30cm)

MATERIALS

1 pair US 5 (3.75mm/no.9) needles
1 US 5 (3.75mm/no.9) circular
   needle 24in (60cm)

Colorway 1 (main picture, front)

Yarn

Rowan Handknit DK cotton
1¾oz (50g) balls
   lime (A)   1
   pale yellow (B)   1
   blue (C)   1

Zip

10in (25cm) zip

Colorway 2 (main picture, back)

Yarn

Rowan Handknit DK cotton
1¾oz (50g) balls
   purple (A)   1
   pale yellow (B)   1
   green (C)   1

Zip

10in (25cm) zip

GAUGE (TENSION)

22 sts and 30 rows to 4in (10cm)
measured over stockinette
(stocking) stitch using US 5
(3.75mm/no.9) needles.

ABBREVIATIONS

See also page 127.
Note: The front panel of the cushion is knitted in three vertical strips that are sewn together to create a square panel. The back panel is striped and knitted in one piece.

TECHNIQUES

Intarsia knitting, see page 119.
Stripes using dp needles,
   see page 120.
Blocking and pressing,
   see page 124.
Fitting a zip, see page 124.
Sewing up, see page 125.

KNIT

Front Panel

Strip one (work two)
Cast on 23 sts using US 5
(3.75mm/no.9) circular needle
and yarn A.
Textured star
✳ Beg with a K row, work 30 rows
in patt from chart for textured star,
ending with a WS row✳
Stockinette (stocking) stitch patt
Work 30 rows in stripe patt in the
foll sequence:
ROW 1 (RS): Yarn B, knit.
ROW 2: Yarn B, purl.
ROW 3: Yarn C, knit.
ROW 4: Yarn C, purl.
Rep these 4 rows six times more,
then work rows 1 and 2 once

more, ending with a WS row.
(30 rows of stripe patt completed)
Textured star
Work from ✳ to ✳.
Bind (cast) off sts.

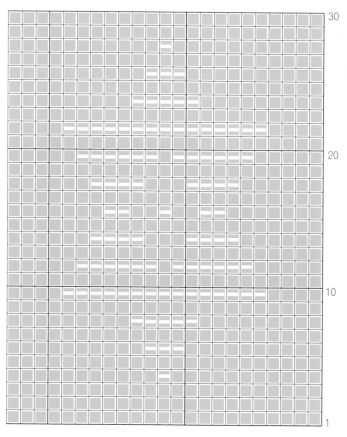

TEXTURED STAR CHART

Key

▢ lime (A)

☐ K on RS, P on WS

⊟ P on RS, K on WS

Strip two (work one)

Cast on 23 sts using US 5 (3.75mm/no.9) circular needle and yarn C.

Reverse stockinette (stocking) stitch patt

Work 30 rows in stripe patt in the foll sequence:

ROW 1 (RS): **Yarn C, purl.**
ROW 2: **Yarn C, knit.**
ROW 3: **Yarn C, purl.**
ROW 4: **Yarn B, knit.**
ROW 5: **Yarn B, purl.**
ROW 6: **Yarn B, knit.**

Rep the 6-row stripe patt four times more, ending with a WS row.

Outline star

Beg with a K row, work 30 rows in patt from chart for outline star, ending with a WS row.

Reverse stockinette (stocking) stitch patt

Work 30 rows in stripe patt in the foll sequence:

ROW 1 (RS): **Yarn B, knit.**
ROW 2: **Yarn B, knit.**
ROW 3: **Yarn B, purl.**
ROW 4: **Yarn C, knit.**
ROW 5: **Yarn C, purl.**
ROW 6: **Yarn C, knit.**
ROW 7: **Yarn B, purl.**

Rep the rows 2–7 three times, then work rows 2–6 once more, ending with a WS row.
Bind (cast) off sts.

Joining strips

Darn in the ends on the WS of the work. With the WS facing, using a damp cloth and a moderate iron, lightly press the strips.

Stitch the strips neatly together placing strip 2 between the other two strips.

Back Panel

With RS of front panel facing and using US 5 (3.75mm/no.9) circular needle and yarn B, pick up and knit 65 sts along the cast on edge of front panel. This pick-up row is

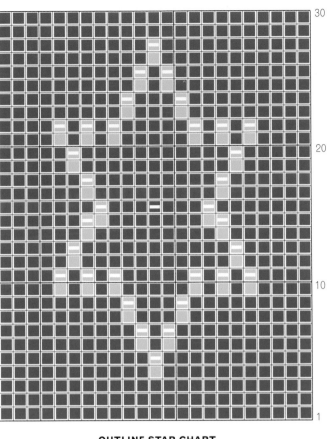

OUTLINE STAR CHART

the first row of the stripe patt repeat.

ROW 1 (RS): **Yarn B, knit.**
ROW 2 (WS): **Yarn B, purl.**
ROW 3: **Yarn B, knit.**
ROW 4: **Yarn C, purl.**
ROW 5: **Yarn C, knit.**
ROW 6: **Yarn C, purl.**
ROW 7: **Yarn B, knit.**
ROW 8: **Yarn B, purl.**
ROW 9: **Yarn B, knit.**
ROW 10: **Yarn A, purl.**
ROW 11: **Yarn A, purl.**
ROW 12: **Yarn C, purl.**
ROW 13: **Yarn C, knit.**
ROW 14: **Yarn C, purl.**
ROW 15: **Yarn A, knit.**
ROW 16: **Yarn A, knit.**

Rep rows 1–16 four times more.
Work rows 1–9 once more.
Bind (cast) off sts
(89 rows)

Key

- ■ blue (C)
- ☐ lime (A)
- ☐ K on RS, P on WS
- ⊟ P on RS, K on WS

COLORWAY 1

FINISHING

Darn in ends on the WS of the work. With WS facing and using a damp pressing cloth and a moderate iron, lightly press the back panel.

Sew top edges of the front and back panels together.

With RS facing, sew zip neatly into opening on right-hand side, ensuring that it sits centrally along this edge. Leave the ends of the work free either side of the zip. Sew these seams together after the zip is fitted, with seam on the outside of the work using a running stitch.

Sew together other side seam.

COLORWAY 2

Patchwork quilt

The ancient craft of piecing together odds and ends of fabric to make bedspreads, blankets and other soft furnishings has always intrigued me. So many diverse effects can be created by simply rearranging the blocks in a different order. This design is made up from one block which is repeated twenty-five times and pieced together to produce a busy geometric pattern. The lines of purl stitches across each block simulate the lines of stitching that are added either by hand or machine to some traditional patchwork quilts.

SIZE
16in × 16in (40cm × 40cm)

MATERIALS
1 pair US 2/3 (3mm/no.11) needles
1 pair US 2 (2.75mm/no.12) needles

Colorway 1 (main picture)
Yarn
Rowan Glace Cotton
1¾oz (50g) balls

mid blue (A)	4
dark red (B)	2
light beige (C)	2
navy (D)	2

Buttons
milk ceramic	3
simply red ceramic	3

Colorway 2
Yarn
Rowan Glace Cotton
1¾oz (50g) balls

mid blue (A)	4
pink (B)	2
palest pink (C)	2
blue (D)	2

Buttons
milk ceramic	3
simply pink ceramic	3

GAUGE (TENSION)
25 sts and 34 rows to 4in (10cm) measured over stockinette (stocking) stitch using US 2/3 (3mm/no.11) needles.

ABBREVIATIONS
See page 127.

Colorway 3
Yarn
Rowan Glace Cotton
1¾oz (50g) balls

purple (A)	4
green (B)	2
yellow (C)	2
dark red (D)	2

Buttons
simply yellow ceramic	3
simply green ceramic	3

TECHNIQUES
Intarsia knitting, see page 119.
Buttonholes, see page 123.
Blocking and pressing, see page 124.
Sewing up, see page 125.

KNIT
Front Panel
The front panel is made up of 25 individual squares that are pieced together to create one panel. You will need to knit the foll numbers of squares:

Block 1 (make 9)
Using US 2/3 (3mm/no.11) needles cast on 23 sts in the foll sequence:
Yarn C, 7 sts
Yarn B, 9 sts
Yarn A, 7 sts
Beg with a RS row and starting with chart row 1, work until 31 rows completed.
Bind (cast) off sts.

Key
■ mid blue (A)

■ dark red (B)

□ light beige (C)

■ navy (D)

□ K on RS, P on WS

⊟ P on RS, K on WS

Block 2 (make 8)
Using US 2/3 (3mm/no.11) needles cast on 23 sts in the foll sequence:
Yarn C, 7 sts
Yarn D, 9 sts
Yarn A, 7 sts
Beg with a RS row and starting with chart row 1, work until 31 rows completed.
Bind (cast) off sts.

Key
■ mid blue (A)

■ navy (D)

□ light beige (C)

■ dark red (B)

□ K on RS, P on WS

⊟ P on RS, K on WS

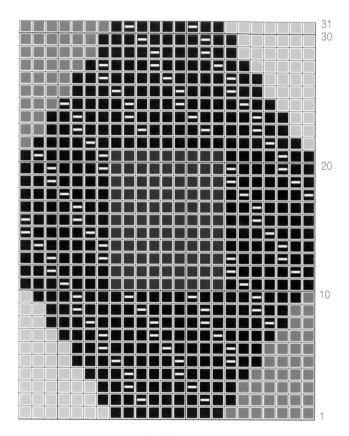

BLOCK 2

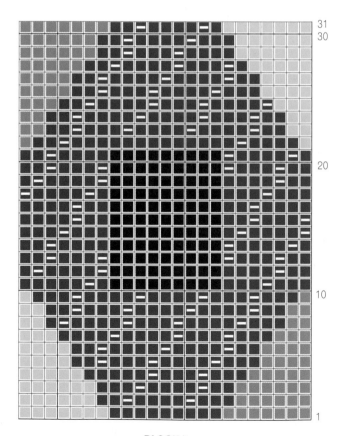

BLOCK 1

Block 3 (make 4)
Using US 2/3 (3mm/no.11) needles
cast on 23 sts in the foll
sequence:
Yarn B, 7 sts
Yarn C, 9 sts
Yarn D, 7 sts
Beg with a RS row and starting
with chart row 1, work until 31 rows
completed.
Bind (cast) off sts.

Key
■ navy (D)

☐ light beige (C)

■ dark red (B)

■ mid blue (A)

☐ K on RS, P on WS

⊟ P on RS, K on WS

Block 4 (make 4)
Using US 2/3 (3mm/no.11) needles
cast on 23 sts in the foll
sequence:
Yarn B, 7 sts
Yarn A, 9 sts
Yarn D, 7 sts
Beg with a RS row and starting
with chart row 1, work until
31 rows completed.
Bind (cast) off sts.

Key
■ navy (D)

■ mid blue (A)

■ dark red (B)

☐ light beige (C)

☐ K on RS, P on WS

⊟ P on RS, K on WS

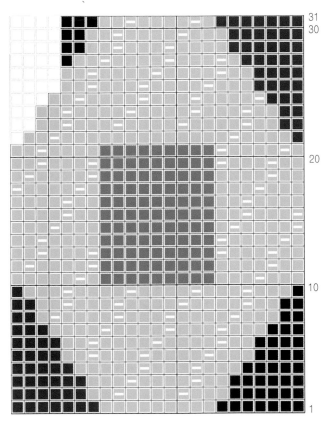

BLOCK 3

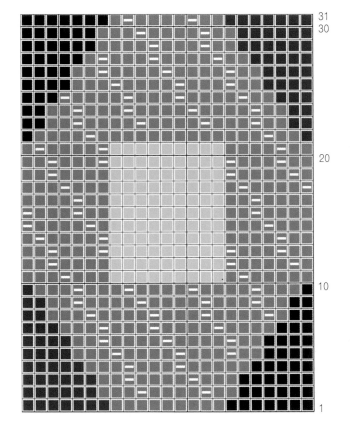

BLOCK 4

Finishing the Front Panel

Using the piecing diagram as a guide, carefully sew together the squares.

Darn the ends in on the WS of the work.

With WS facing, press the front panel using a damp pressing cloth and a warm iron.

Tip: An alternative and easier way to piece together the front panel is as folls. After you have completed a square and the stitches are bound (cast) off, begin the next square above it by picking up the required number of stitches along the bound (cast) off edge of the previous square. Remember that the pick up row is the first row of the chart. Repeat this with each square until a strip is completed.

The sewing together of the individual squares stitch by stitch is avoided and you will only have the vertical seams to sew together to complete the front panel of the cushion.

Buttonhole Panel

With RS facing and using a US 2 (2.75mm/no.12) needle and yarn B, pick up and knit 108 sts along the bound (cast) off edge of the front panel.

✳✳NEXT ROW (WS): Knit.

Slip sts back onto left-hand needle so that the WS is facing you again.

Change to US 2/3 (3mm/no.11) needles.

Using yarn A, purl 1 row.

4-row seed (moss) stitch patt repeat

Yarn A only.

ROW 1 (RS): K3, [P2, K2] twenty-five times, P2, K3.

ROW 2 (WS): P3, [K2, P2] twenty-five times, K2, P3.

ROWS 3: P3, [K2, P2] twenty-five times, K2, P3.
ROW 4: K3, [P2, K2] twenty-five times, P2, K3.
Rep the 4-row patt repeat eighteen times.
(72 rows, not including the purl row at the beginning.)✳✳

Buttonhole band

Change to US 2 (2.75mm/no.12) needles.
NEXT ROW (RS): K3, [P2, K2] twenty-five times, P2, K3.
NEXT ROW (WS): P3, [K2, P2] twenty-five times, K2, P3.
Rep the last 2 rows once more.
NEXT ROW (RS) (BUTTONHOLE ROW): K3, P2, bind (cast) off next 3 sts, P1 (this is the st already on the needle), [K2, P2] three times, K2, P1, bind (cast) off next 3 sts, [P2, K2] four times including st already on the needle, bind (cast) off next 3 sts, K1 (this is the st already on the needle), [P2, K2] three times, P2, K1, bind (cast) off next 3 sts, [K2, P2] four times including st already on the needle, bind (cast) off next 3 sts, P1 (this is the st already on the needle), [K2, P2] three times, K2, P1, bind (cast) off next 3 sts, P2 (including st already on the needle), K3.
NEXT ROW (WS): P3, K2, turn work (RS facing), cast on 3 sts, turn work again (WS facing), K1, [P2, K2] three times, P2, K1, turn work (RS facing), cast on 3 sts, turn work again (WS facing), [K2, P2] four times, turn work (RS facing), cast on 3 sts, turn work again (WS facing), P1, [K2, P2] three times, K2, P1, turn work (RS facing), cast on 3 sts, turn work again (WS facing), [P2, K2] four times, turn work (RS facing), cast on 3 sts, turn work again (WS facing), K1, [P2, K2] three times, P2, K1, turn work (RS facing), cast on 3 sts, turn work again (WS facing), K2, P3.
NEXT ROW (RS): K3, [P2, K2]

twenty-five times, P2, K3.
NEXT ROW (WS): P3, [K2, P2] twenty-five times, K2, P3.
NEXT ROW (RS): K3, [P2, K2] twenty-five times, P2, K3.
With WS facing, bind (cast) off sts knitwise.

Buttonband Panel

With RS facing and using a US 2 (2.75mm/no.12) needle and yarn D, pick up and knit 108 sts along the cast on edge of the front panel.
Rep patt instructions for buttonhole panel from ✳✳ to ✳✳.

Buttonband

NEXT ROW (RS): K3, [P2, K2] twenty-five times, P2, K3.
NEXT ROW (WS): P3, [K2, P2] twenty-five times, K2, P3.
Rep the last 2 rows seven times more.
With RS facing, bind (cast) off sts.

FINISHING

Darn in ends on the WS of the work. With WS facing and using a damp pressing cloth and a moderate iron lightly press the cushion cover.

Mark the center point along side seam edges of front panel. Sew side seams of buttonhole panel to front panel ensuring that buttonholes are in line with the marked center point.

Sew side seams of buttonband panel to front panel, inserting the broad rib stitch border at finished edge under the finished edge of the buttonhole panel, and sew down into place.

Turn cover inside out and press seams.

Sew buttons onto buttonband to correspond with buttonholes.

Log cabin

Log Cabin is the name of a traditional patchwork block which is created by sewing together strips of fabric to make a square. My knitted interpretation of this much-loved patchwork is made up of nine separate blocks. You can experiment with the order of piecing yourself and create a totally different look or add more blocks to the design to make a larger cushion-cover. Just have fun!

SIZE
12in × 12in (30cm × 30cm)

MATERIALS
1 pair US 2/3 (3mm/no.11) needles
1 pair US 2 (2.75mm/no.12) needles

Yarn
Rowan Glace Cotton
1¾oz (50g) balls

dark pink (A)	2
cream (B)	1
mid pink (C)	3
bright blue (D)	1
pale pink (E)	1
purple (F)	1
lilac (G)	1
blue (H)	1

Buttons
pink hearts ceramic	5

GAUGE (TENSION)
25 sts and 34 rows to 4in (10cm) measured over stockinette (stocking) stitch using US 2/3 (3mm/no.11) needles.

ABBREVIATIONS
See page 127.

TECHNIQUES
Intarsia knitting, see page 119.
Buttonholes, see page 123.
Blocking and pressing,
   see page 124.
Sewing up, see page 125.

KNIT

Front Panel

The front panel is made up of 9 individual squares that are pieced together to create one panel.

You will need to knit the foll numbers of squares:

Block 1 (make 4)

Cast on 30 sts using US 2/3 (3mm/no.11) needles and yarn A. Beg with a RS row and starting with chart row 1, work until 42 rows completed.
Bind (cast) off sts.

Key

■ dark pink (A)

□ cream (B)

■ mid pink (C)

■ bright blue (D)

■ pale pink (E)

■ purple (F)

■ lilac (G)

■ blue (H)

□ K on RS, P on WS

⊟ P on RS, K on WS

Block 2 (make 2)

Using US 2/3 (3mm/no.11) needles cast on 30 sts in the foll sequence:
Yarn D, 5 sts
Yarn A, 25 sts
Beg with a RS row and starting with chart row 1, work until 42 rows completed.
Bind (cast) off sts.

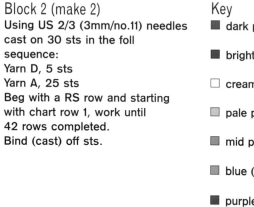

Key

■ dark pink (A)

■ bright blue (D)

□ cream (B)

■ pale pink (E)

■ mid pink (C)

■ blue (H)

■ purple (F)

■ lilac (G)

□ K on RS, P on WS

⊟ P on RS, K on WS

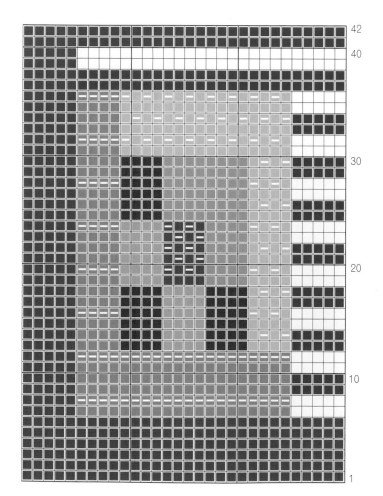

BLOCK 1

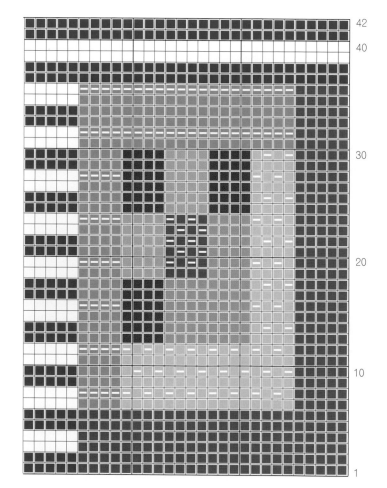

BLOCK 2

Block 3 (make 2)

Cast on 30 sts using US 2/3 (3mm/no.11) needles and yarn D. Beg with a RS row and starting with chart row 1, work until 42 rows completed. Bind (cast) off sts.

Key

- ■ bright blue (D)
- □ cream (B)
- ■ mid pink (C)
- ■ dark pink (A)
- ■ pale pink (E)
- ■ purple (F)
- ■ lilac (G)
- ■ blue (H)

- □ K on RS, P on WS
- ⊟ P on RS, K on WS

Block 4 (make 1)

Using US 2/3 (3mm/no.11) needles cast on 30 sts in the foll sequence:
Yarn D, 25 sts
Yarn A, 5 sts
Beg with a RS row and starting with chart row 1, work until 42 rows completed. Bind (cast) off sts.

Key

- ■ dark pink (A)
- ■ bright blue (D)
- □ cream (B)
- ■ mid pink (C)
- ■ pale pink (E)
- ■ purple (F)
- ■ blue (H)
- ■ lilac (G)

- □ K on RS, P on WS
- ⊟ P on RS, K on WS

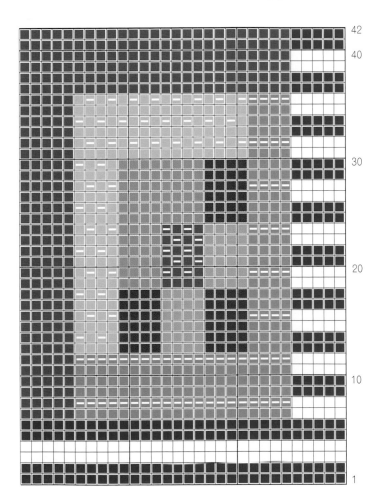

BLOCK 3

BLOCK 4

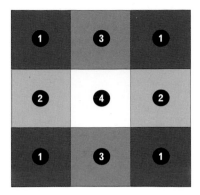

Finishing the Front Panel

Using the piecing diagram above as a guide, carefully sew together the squares.

Darn the ends in on the WS of the work. With WS facing, press the front panel using a damp pressing cloth and a warm iron.

Tip: An alternative and easier way to piece together the front panel is as folls: After you have completed a square and the stitches are bound (cast) off, begin the next square above it by picking up the required number of stitches along the bound (cast) off edge of the previous square. Remember that the pick up row is the first row of the chart. Repeat this with each square until a strip is completed.

The sewing together of the individual squares stitch by stitch is avoided, and you will only have the vertical seams to sew together to complete the front panel of the cushion.

Buttonhole Panel

With RS facing and using a US 2 (2.75mm/no.12) needle and yarn E, pick up and knit 84 sts along the bound (cast) off (top) edge of the front panel.

NEXT ROW (WS): Knit.
Change to US 2/3 (3mm/no.11) needles.
Beg with a RS row, cont to work from buttonhole panel chart until chart row 36 completed.

Buttonhole band
ROW 1 (RS): Yarn D, knit.
ROW 2 (WS): Yarn D, P41, P2tog, P41.
(83 sts)
ROW 3: Yarn B, knit.
ROW 4: Yarn B, purl.

Key

■ bright blue (D)	□ K on RS, P on WS
▨ pale pink (E)	
▩ mid pink (C)	⊟ P on RS, K on WS
□ cream (B)	
▨ blue (H)	
■ dark pink (A)	

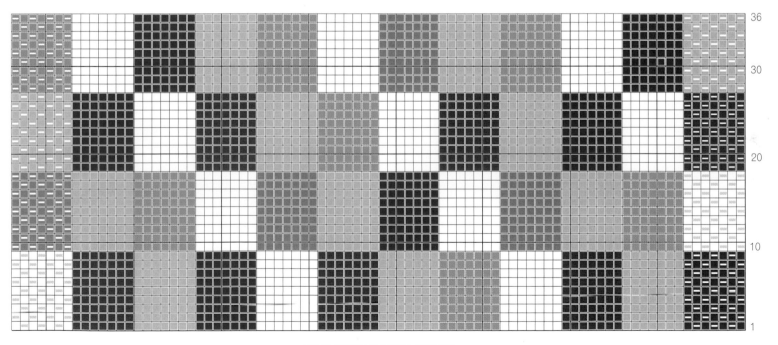

BUTTONHOLE PANEL CHART

ROW 5 (RS) (BUTTONHOLE ROW):
Yarn D, K4, [bind (cast) off next 3 sts, K15 including st already on needle] four times, bind (cast) off next 3 sts, K4 including st already on needle.

ROW 6: Yarn D, P4, [turn work (RS facing), cast on 3 sts, turn work again (WS facing), P15] four times, turn work (WS facing), cast on 3 sts, turn work again (RS facing), P4.

ROWS 7–8: Rep rows 3–4.

ROW 9: Rep row 1.

With WS facing and using yarn D, bind (cast) off sts knitwise.

Buttonband Panel

With RS facing and using a US 2 (2.75mm/no.12) needle and yarn E, pick up and knit 87 sts along the cast on edge of the front panel.

NEXT ROW (WS): Knit.

Change to US 2/3 (3mm/no.11) needles.

Using yarn C and beg with a RS row, work 2 rows in stockinette (stocking) stitch.

2-row rib patt repeat

Yarn C only.

ROW 1 (RS): [K1, P1] three times, [K5, (P1, K1) twice, P1] eight times, K1.

ROW 2 (WS): [K1, P1] twice, K1, [P7, K1, P1, K1] seven times, P7, [K1, P1] twice, K1.

Rep the 2-row patt repeat fifty-six times in total.

(114 rows including the 2 stockinette (stocking) stitch rows at the beginning.)

Buttonband

Change to US 2 (2.75mm/no.12) needles.

Top edge

ROW 1 (RS): [K1, P1] to last st, K1.

ROW 2 (WS): [K1, P1] to last st, K1.

Rep the last 2 rows five times more.

Bind (cast) off sts.

FINISHING

Darn in ends on the WS of the work. With WS facing and using a damp pressing cloth and a moderate iron, lightly press the buttonhole and buttonband panels. Sew side seams.

Turn cover inside out and press seams.

Sew buttons onto buttonband to correspond with buttonholes.

Playtime

Crayons

Big, chunky wax crayons are used by many young children to create their first pieces of artwork. The naïveté of their drawings and the bold colors of the crayons were the inspiration for this cheerful design. Soft, ribbed cables in vibrant shades are set against a cool, pale-blue background to create an eye-catching and cuddly cushion cover.

SIZE

16in × 16in (40cm × 40cm)

MATERIALS

1 pair US 10.5 (7mm/no.2) needles
1 pair US 10.5 (6.5mm/no.3) needles
1 US 10.5 (7mm/no.2) circular
    needle 24in (60cm)
Cable needle

Yarn

Rowan Cork
1¾oz (50g) balls

pale blue (A)	3
purple (B)	2
magenta (C)	2
lime (D)	2
orange (E)	2

Buttons

simply purple ceramic	2
simply pink ceramic	2
simply blue ceramic	1
simply green ceramic	1

GAUGE (TENSION)

15 sts and 22 rows to 4in (10cm) measured over stockinette (stocking) stitch using US 10.5 (7mm/no.2) needles.

ABBREVIATIONS

c14b = slip next 7 sts onto cable needle and hold at back of work, [K1, P1] three times, K1, then work the stitches on the cable needle as folls: [K1, P1] three times, K1.
Note: To keep the color changes neat, pull firmly on the yarns when changing color before and after the cabled stitches.
See also page 127.

TECHNIQUES

Cables, see page 122.
Intarsia knitting, see page 119.
Stripes using dp needles,
    see page 120.
Buttonholes, see page 123.
Blocking and pressing,
    see page 124.
Sewing up, see page 125.

KNIT

Front Panel

Cast on 63 sts using US 10.5 (7mm/no.2) needles in the foll sequence:
Yarn A, 3 sts.
Yarn B, 7 sts.
Yarn A, 3 sts.
Yarn C, 7 sts.
Yarn A, 3 sts.
Yarn D, 7 sts.
Yarn A, 3 sts.
Yarn B, 7 sts.
Yarn A, 3 sts.
Yarn E, 7 sts.
Yarn A, 3 sts.
Yarn D, 7 sts.
Yarn A, 3 sts.

NEXT ROW (WS): K3A, P7D, K3A, P7E, K3A, P7B, K3A, P7D, K3A, P7C, K3A, P7B, K3A.
NEXT ROW (INC) (RS): Keeping colors as set in last row [P3, inc once into each of the next 7 sts] six times, P3.
(105 sts)
NEXT ROW (SETTING THE STS IN PATT) (WS): [K3, (P1, K1) three times, P2, (K1, P1) three times] six times, K3.
14-row cable patt repeat
ROW 1 (RS): [P3, (K1, P1) three times, K2, (P1, K1) three times] six times, P3.
ROW 2 (WS): [K3, (P1, K1) three times, P2, (K1, P1) three times] six times, K3.
ROWS 3–12: Rep rows 1–2 five times.
ROW 13: [P3, c14b] six times, P3.
ROW 14: As row 2.
Rep the 14-row cable patt repeat until work measures 16in (40cm) square, ending with a WS row.
NEXT ROW (DEC) (RS): Keeping colors as set: [P3, K2tog seven times] six times, P3.
(63 sts)
Bind (cast) off sts.
Mark the center point along side seams of front panel.

Buttonhole Panel

With RS facing using a US 10.5 (6.5mm/no.3) needle and yarn A, pick up and knit 63 sts along bound (cast) off edge of front panel.

NEXT ROW (WS): Knit.

Change to US 10.5 (7mm/no.2) circular needle.

11-row stripe patt repeat worked in stockinette (stocking) stitch

Yarn A, 5 rows.

Yarn C, 6 rows.

Beg with a RS row, rep the 11-row stripe patt repeat until work is 5 rows shorter than to marked center points along side edges of front panel, ending with a RS row.

Buttonhole band

Change to US 10.5 (6.5mm/no.3) needles.

NEXT ROW (WS): Yarn B, purl.

NEXT ROW (RS): Yarn B, [K1, P1] to last st, K1.

NEXT ROW (WS): Yarn B, [P1, K1] to last st, P1.

NEXT ROW (RS): Yarn B, [K1, P1] to last st, K1.

NEXT ROW (WS) (BUTTONHOLE ROW): Yarn B, P1, K1, P1, [bind (cast) off next 2 sts, (K1, P1) four times including st already on the needle, K1, bind (cast) off next 2 sts, (P1, K1) four times including st already on the needle, P1] twice, bind (cast) off next 2 sts, [K1, P1] four times including st already on the needle, K1, bind (cast) off next 2 sts, P1, K1, P1 Including st already on the needle.

NEXT ROW (RS): Yarn B, K1, P1, K1, [turn work (RS facing), cast on 2 sts, turn work again (WS facing), (P1, K1) four times, P1, turn work (RS facing), cast on 2 sts, turn work again (WS facing), (K1, P1) four times, K1] twice, turn work (RS facing), cast on 2 sts, turn work again (WS facing), [P1, K1] four times, P1, turn work (RS facing), cast on 2 sts, turn work again (WS facing), K1, P1, K1.

NEXT ROW (WS): Yarn B, [P1, K1] to last st, P1.

NEXT ROW (RS): Yarn B, [K1, P1] to last st, K1.

With WS facing, bind (cast) off sts knitwise using yarn D.

Buttonband Panel

With RS facing, using a US 10.5 (6.5mm/no.3) needle and yarn A, pick up and knit 63 sts along cast on edge of front panel.

NEXT ROW (WS): Knit.

Change to US 10.5 (7mm/no.2) circular needle.

11-row stripe patt repeat worked in stockinette (stocking) stitch

Yarn A, 5 rows.

Yarn E, 6 rows.

Beg with a RS row, rep the 11-row stripe patt repeat until work matches to marked center points along side edges of front panel, ending with a WS row.

Buttonband

Change to US 10.5 (6.5mm/no.3) needles.

Cont in stripe patt repeat for a further 8 rows.

Bind (cast) off sts.

FINISHING

Darn in ends on the WS of the work. With WS facing and using a damp pressing cloth and a cool iron, lightly press the cushion cover.

Sew side seams of buttonhole panel to front panel ensuring that buttonholes are in line with the marked center point.

Sew side seams of buttonband panel to front panel, inserting broad stockinette (stocking) stitch border at finished edge under the finished edge of the buttonhole panel, and sew down into place.

Turn cover inside out and press seams.

Sew buttons onto buttonband to correspond with buttonholes.

Bobble cube

This bright and colorful fun cube gives children something tactile to play with. Each side of the cube is knitted in a different color with bright contrasting bobbles. If the sponge used to fill the cushion cover is sturdy enough, the cube can be used by small children as a seat.

SIZE
11½in × 11½in × 11½in
(29cm × 29cm × 29cm) cube

MATERIALS
1 pair US 5 (3.75mm/no.9) needles

Yarn
Rowan Wool Cotton
1¾oz (50g) balls

purple (A)	2
orange (B)	2
blue (C)	2
yellow (D)	2
green (E)	2
pink (F)	2

Zip
10in (25cm) concealed zip

GAUGE (TENSION)
24 sts and 32 rows to 4in (10cm) measured over stockinette (stocking) stitch using US 5 (3.75mm/no.9) needles.

ABBREVIATIONS
mb = **make bobble:** knit into front, back, front, back, front, back of next stitch, [turn work (WS facing), P6, turn work again (RS facing), K6] twice, slip 2nd, 3rd, 4th, 5th and 6th sts off over 1st st, pull firmly on yarn to tighten bobble.
See also page 127.

TECHNIQUES
Darning in ends, see page 120.
Fitting a zip, see page 124.
Sewing up, see page 125.

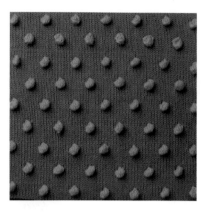

KNIT
Panel 1
Cast on 69 sts using US 5 (3.75mm/no.9) needles and yarn A. Beg with a RS row, work 5 rows in stockinette (stocking) stitch.
✳✳NEXT ROW (WS): P4A, [P1B, P9A] six times, P1B, P4A.
20-row bobble patt repeat
ROW 1 (RS): K4A, [mb (yarn B), K9A] six times, mb (yarn B), K4A.
ROW 2 (WS): Yarn A, purl.
ROW 3 (RS): Yarn A, knit.
ROWS 4–9: Rep rows 2–3 three times.
ROW 10: P9A, [P1B, P9A] five times, P1B, P9A.
ROW 11: K9A, [mb (yarn B), K9A] five times, mb (yarn B), K9A.
ROWS 12–19: Rep rows 2–3 four times.
ROW 20: P4A, [P1B, P9A] six times, P1B, P4A.
Rep the 20 row patt repeat four times in total.
Rep rows 1–6 once more.
Bind (cast) off sts.
(92 rows)✳✳

Panel 2
With RS facing and using a US 5 (3.75mm/no,9) needle and yarn C, pick up and knit 69 sts along bound (cast) off edge of panel 1.
NEXT ROW (WS): Purl.
Work 3 rows in stockinette (stocking) stitch.
Rep patt instructions for panel 1 from ✳✳ to ✳✳, but use yarn C in place of yarn A and yarn D in place of yarn B.

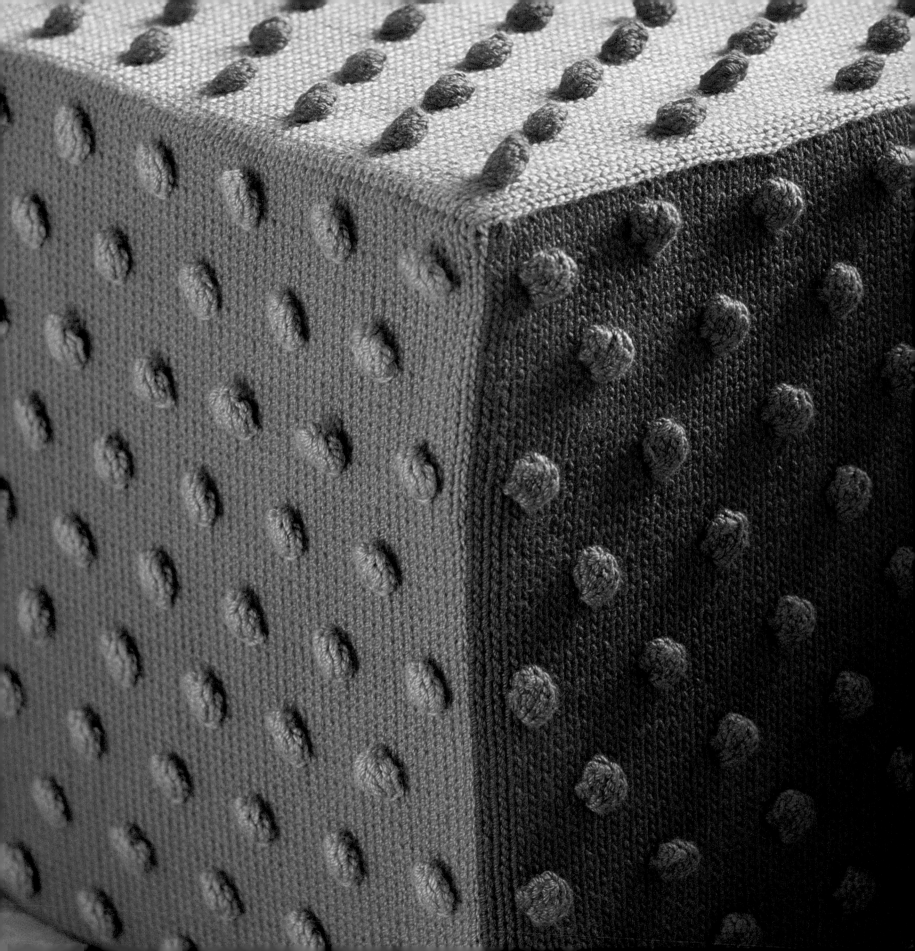

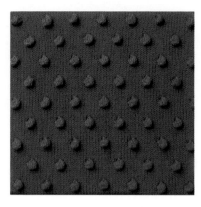

Panel 3

With RS facing and using a US 5 (3.75mm/no,9) needle and yarn E, pick up and knit 69 sts along cast on edge of panel 1.

NEXT ROW (WS): **Purl.**

Work 3 rows in stockinette (stocking) stitch.

Rep patt instructions for panel 1 from ✱✱ to ✱✱, but use yarn E in place of yarn A and yarn F in place of yarn B.

Panel 4

With RS facing and using a US 5 (3.75mm/no,9) needle and yarn B, pick up and knit 69 sts along bound (cast) off edge of panel 3.

NEXT ROW (WS): **Purl.**

Work 3 rows in stockinette (stocking) stitch.

Rep patt instructions for panel 1 from ✱✱ to ✱✱, but use yarn B in place of yarn A and yarn C in place of yarn B.

Panel 5

With RS facing and using a US 5 (3.75mm/no,9) needle and yarn D, pick up and knit 69 sts along left-hand side edge of panel 3.

NEXT ROW (WS): **Purl.**

Work 3 rows in stockinette (stocking) stitch.

Rep patt instructions for panel 1 from ✱✱ to ✱✱, but use yarn D in place of yarn A and yarn E in place of yarn B.

Panel 6

With RS facing and using a US 5 (3.75mm/no,9) needle and yarn F, pick up and knit 69 sts along right-hand side edge of panel 3.

NEXT ROW (WS): **Purl.**

Work 3 rows in stockinette (stocking) stitch.

Rep patt instructions for panel 1 from ✱✱ to ✱✱, but use yarn F in place of yarn A and yarn A in place of yarn B.

FINISHING

It is easier to sew the cushion cover together around the pad. Do not press panels.

Darn in ends on the WS of the work.

Lay the panels out flat with WS facing up. Position the cube pad on panel 3.

Wrap cover over cube pad. With RS facing, sew zip neatly in between finished edges of panels 2 and 4, ensuring that it sits centrally along this edge. Leave the ends of the work free either side of the zip. Sew these seams together after the zip is fitted, with seam on the outside of the work using a running stitch.

Sew together all other seams.

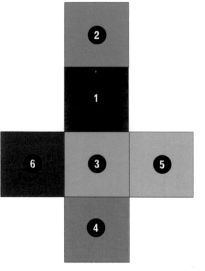

Fun and games

In this design the popular children's game of Tick-Tack-Toe (Noughts and Crosses) is translated into a beaded pattern. Letters and numbers in bright colors are embroidered around a central panel to create a cushion that is educational as well as fun!

SIZE
14in × 14in (35cm × 35cm)

MATERIALS
1 pair US 5 (3.75mm/no.9) needles
1 pair US 3 (3.25mm/no.10) needles

Yarn
Rowan Handknit DK Cotton
1¾oz (50g) balls

blue (A)	3
green (B)	2
yellow (C)	1
red (D)	2

Beads
⅛in (4mm) pebble beads

red	120 approx.
blue	123 approx.

Buttons
blue speckle (matte) ceramic	5

GAUGE (TENSION)
22 sts and 30 rows to 4in (10cm) measured over stockinette (stocking) stitch using US 5 (3.75mm/no.9) needles.

ABBREVIATIONS
In this pattern, the beads are knitted on reverse stockinette (stocking) stitch.
pb = place bead: keeping yarn at front of work, sl1 purlwise, slide bead up so that it is sitting in front of the slipped st, keeping yarn at front of work pull firmly so that bead sits snugly.
See also page 127.

TECHNIQUES
Knitting with beads, see page 121.
Adding embroidery to knitting, see page 124.
Buttonholes, see page 123.
Darning in ends, see page 120.
Blocking and pressing, see page 124.
Sewing up, see page 125.
Note: It is advisable to Swiss darn the numbers and letters onto the front panel after knitting.

KNIT
Front Panel
Cast on 75 sts using US 5 (3.75mm/no.9) needles and yarn A. Beg with a RS row and row 1 of the chart, work until 104 chart rows completed.
Bind (cast) off sts.

Buttonhole Panel
Thread blue beads onto yarn D. With RS facing and using a US 3 (3.25mm/no.10) needle and yarn

D, pick up and knit 75 sts along bound (cast) off edge of front panel.
NEXT ROW (WS): Knit.
✱✱Change to US 5 (3.75mm/no.9) needles.
NEXT ROW (RS): Knit.
NEXT ROW (WS): [K1, P1] twice, [(K3, P1) three times, K1, P1] five times, K1.
6-row seed (moss) stitch and bead patt repeat

ROW 1 (RS): [K1, P1] twice, [P3, yb, sl1 purlwise, yf, P1, pb, P1, yb, sl1 purlwise, yf, P4, K1, P1] five times, K1.
ROW 2 (WS): [K1, P1] twice, [(K3, P1) three times, K1, P1] five times, K1.
ROW 3: [K1, P1] twice, [(P3, yb, sl1 purlwise, yf) twice, P4, K1, P1] five times, K1.
ROW 4: [K1, P1] twice, [K3, P1, K1, pb, K1, P1, K3, P1, K1, P1] five times, K1.

Key

■ blue (A)

■ green (B)

□ yellow (C)

■ red (D)

● red bead

● blue bead

□ K on RS, P on WS

⊟ P on RS, K on WS

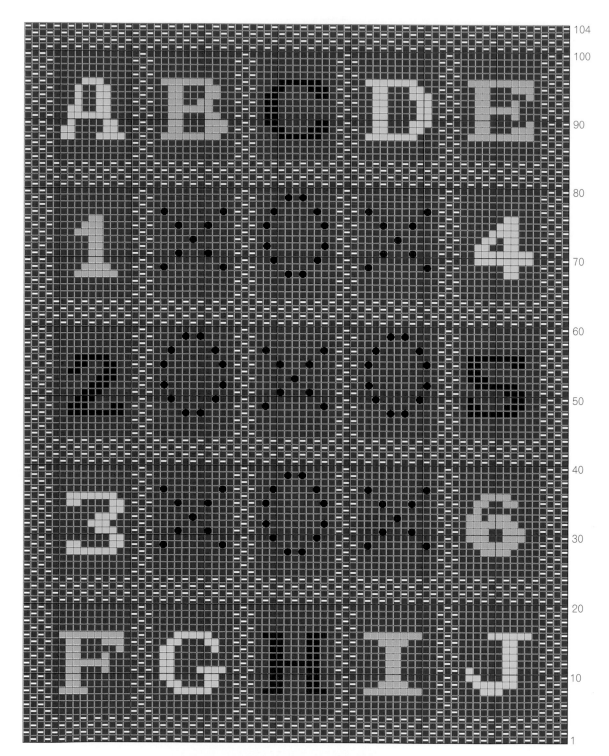

TICK-TACK-TOE (NOUGHTS AND CROSSES) CHART

ROW 5: **As row 3.**

ROW 6: **As row 2.**

Rep the 6 row patt repeat seven times.

Rep rows 1–3 once more, ending with a RS row.✱✱

Buttonhole band

Change to US 3 (3.25mm/no.10) needles.

NEXT ROW (WS): **[K1, P1] thirty-seven times, K1.**

NEXT ROW (RS): **[K1, P1] thirty-seven times, K1.**

Rep the last 2 rows once more.

NEXT ROW (WS) (BUTTONHOLE ROW): **[K1, P1] twice, [bind (cast) off next 3 sts, (P1, K1) six times including st already on needle, P1] four times, bind (cast) off next 3 sts, [P1, K1] twice, including st already on needle.**

NEXT ROW: **[K1, P1] twice, [turn work (WS facing), cast on 3 sts, turn work again (RS facing), (P1, K1) six times, P1] four times, turn work (WS facing), cast on 3 sts, turn work again (RS facing), [P1, K1] twice.**

NEXT ROW: **[K1, P1] thirty-seven times, K1.**

NEXT ROW: **[K1, P1] thirty-seven times, K1.**

With WS facing and using yarn A, bind (cast) off sts knitwise.

Buttonband Panel

Thread red beads onto yarn B. With RS facing and using a US 3 (3.25mm/no.10) needle and yarn B, pick up and knit 75 sts along cast on edge of front panel.

NEXT ROW (WS): **Knit.**

Rep instructions for buttonhole panel from ✱✱ to ✱✱.

Buttonband

Change to US 3 (3.25mm/no.10) needles.

NEXT ROW (WS): **[K1, P1] thirty-seven times, K1.**

NEXT ROW (RS): **[K1, P1] thirty-seven** times, K1.

Rep the last 2 rows seven times more.

Bind (cast) off sts.

FINISHING

Darn in ends on the WS of the work. With WS facing and using a damp pressing cloth and a moderate iron lightly press the cushion cover.

Mark the center point along the side seam edges of front panel.

Sew side seams of buttonhole panel to front panel, ensuring that buttonholes are in line with the marked center point.

Sew side seams of buttonband panel to front panel, inserting broad seed (moss) stitch border at finished edge under the finished edge of the buttonhole panel, and sew down into place.

Turn cover inside out and press seams.

Sew buttons onto buttonband to correspond with buttonholes.

Rainbow drops

*At our local candy store we used to buy bags of multi-colored candies called **Rainbow Drops**. This design is based on these candies, but I have used brighter colors to create a vibrant, textured stripe pattern that follows the colors of the rainbow. The stripes are embellished with rows of small cube beads which add color and texture to the surface of the knitting, making it a fun and tactile cushion.*

SIZE
16in × 16in (40cm × 40cm)

MATERIALS
1 pair US 2/3 (3mm/no.11) needles
1 pair US 2 (2.75mm/no.12) needles

Yarn
Rowan Glace Cotton
1¾oz (50g) balls

red (A)	2
orange (B)	1
yellow (C)	1
green (D)	1
blue (E)	2
indigo (F)	1
violet (G)	1

Beads
³⁄₁₆ × ³⁄₁₆ × ³⁄₁₆in (4 × 4 × 4mm)
cube beads

red	209
orange	96
yellow	96
green	96
blue	72
indigo	185
violet	72

Buttons

blue speckol (matte) ceramic	6

GAUGE (TENSION)
25 sts and 38 rows to 4in (10cm) measured over striped beaded patt using US 2/3 (3mm/no.11) needles.

ABBREVIATIONS
pb = (RS): with yarn forward, slide bead up yarn, slip 1 stitch purlwise, yarn back leaving bead in front of the slipped stitch.
See also page 127.

TECHNIQUES
Knitting with beads, see page 120.
Buttonholes, see page 123.
Darning in ends, see page 120.
Blocking and pressing,
   see page 124.
Sewing up, see page 125.

KNIT
Front Panel
Note: There are 24 beads on each beaded row (row 5 of the stripe patt repeat).
Thread beads onto yarns before commencing the stripe patt repeat, as folls:
Yarn A, orange beads.
Yarn B, yellow beads.
Yarn C, green beads.
Yarn D, blue beads.
Yarn E, indigo beads.
Yarn F, violet beads.
Yarn G, red beads.

Cast on 101 sts using US 2/3 (3mm/no.11) needles and yarn A.
6-row stripe patt repeat
**ROW 1 (RS): Knit.
ROW 2 (WS): Purl.
ROW 3: Knit.
ROW 4: P2, [K1, P3] twenty-four times, K1, P2.
ROW 5: K4, [pb, K3] twenty-four times, K1.
ROW 6: Purl.

Rep the 6-row patt repeat in the foll sequence:
ROWS 7–12: Yarn B.
ROWS 13–18: Yarn C.
ROWS 19–24: Yarn D.
ROWS 25–30: Yarn E.
ROWS 31–36: Yarn F.
ROWS 37–42: Yarn G. **
Rep from ** to ** twice more.

Rep the sequence for a further 24 rows ending with a green stripe. *(150 rows)*
Bind (cast) off sts.

Buttonhole Panel

With RS facing, using US 2 (2.75mm/no.12) needles and yarn C, pick and knit 101 sts along bound (cast) off edge of front panel.
NEXT ROW (WS): Knit.
Change to 2/3 (3mm/no.11) needles.
Thread indigo beads onto yarn A.
Join in yarn A.
✳✳ Beg with a RS row work 2 rows in stockinette (stocking) stitch.
16-row beaded patt repeat
ROW 1 (RS): Knit.
ROW 2 (WS): P6, [K1, P7] eleven times, K1, P6.
ROW 3: K2, [pb, K7] twelve times, pb, K2.
ROW 4: Purl.
ROW 5: Knit.
ROWS 6–9: Rep rows 4–5 twice.
ROW 10: P2, [K1, P7] twelve times, K1, P2.
ROW 11: K6, [pb, K7] eleven times, pb, K6.
ROW 12: Purl.
ROW 13: Knit.
ROWS 14–15: Rep rows 12–13 once.
ROW 16: Purl.
Rep rows 1–16 four times in total.
Rep rows 1–3 once more ending with a RS row.✳✳
Buttonhole band
Change to US 2 (2.75mm/no.12) needles.
NEXT ROW (WS): Yarn B, purl.
ROW 1 (RS): Yarn B, K4, [(P3, K3] sixteen times, K1.
ROW 2 (WS): Yarn C, P4, [K3, P3] sixteen times, P1.
NEXT ROW: Yarn C, rep row 1.
NEXT ROW: Yarn D, rep row 2.

NEXT ROW: Yarn D, rep row 1.
NEXT ROW (WS) (BUTTONHOLE ROW): Yarn E, P4, [bind (cast) off next 3 sts, P3 including st already on the needle, (K3, P3) twice] five times, bind (cast) off next 3 sts, P4 including st already on the needle.
NEXT ROW (RS): Yarn E, K4, [turn work (WS facing), cast on 3 sts, turn work again (RS facing), K3, (P3, K3) twice] five times, turn work (WS facing), cast on 3 sts, turn work again (RS facing), K4.
NEXT ROW: Yarn F, rep row 2.
NEXT ROW: Yarn F, rep row 1.
NEXT ROW: Yarn G, rep row 2.
NEXT ROW: Yarn G, rep row 1.
With WS facing and using yarn G, bind (cast) off sts knitwise.

Buttonband Panel

With RS facing, using US 2 (2.75mm/no.12) needles and yarn C, pick and knit 101 sts along cast on edge of front panel.
NEXT ROW (WS): Knit.
Change to 2/3 (3mm/no.11) needles.
Thread red beads onto yarn E.
Join in yarn E.
Rep patt instructions for buttonhole panel from ✳✳ to ✳✳.
Buttonband
Change to US 2 (2.75mm/no.12) needles.
Beg with a WS row cont to work in stockinette (stocking) stitch using yarn E only, for a further 15 rows.
Bind (cast) off sts.

FINISHING

Darn in ends on the WS of the work. With WS facing and using a damp pressing cloth and a moderate iron, lightly press the cushion cover.

   Mark the center point along the side seam edges of front panel.

   Sew side seams of buttonhole panel to front panel ensuring that buttonholes are in line with the marked center point.

   Sew side seams of buttonband panel to front panel, inserting broad stockinette (stocking) stitch border at finished edge under the finished edge of the buttonhole panel, and sew down into place.

   Sew buttons onto buttonband to correspond with buttonholes.

Happy flowers

The simple motif of a stylized flower is repeated in this wildly colorful design. A sense of innocence is created by the childlike shape of the flower and the bold colors in which it is knitted. The front panel is knitted in four strips that are pieced together to make one block. This makes it a much easier design to knit than perhaps first thought.

SIZE
14in × 14in (35cm × 35cm)

MATERIALS
1 pair US 5 (3.75mm/no.9) needles
1 pair US 3 (3.25mm/no.10) needles

Yarn
Rowan Wool Cotton
1¾oz (50g) balls

orange (A)	1
aqua (B)	1
pink (C)	2
yellow (D)	2
purple (E)	1
green (F)	1

Buttons

simply green ceramic	2
simply pink ceramic	1
simply blue ceramic	1
simply purple ceramic	1

GAUGE (TENSION)
24 sts and 32 rows to 4in (10cm) measured over stockinette (stocking) stitch using US 5 (3.75mm/no.9) needles.

ABBREVIATIONS
See page 127.

TECHNIQUES
Intarsia knitting, see page 119.
Buttonholes, see page 123.
Darning in ends, see page 120.
Blocking and pressing,
    see page 124.
Sewing up, see page 125.

KNIT
Front Panel
The front panel is worked in 4 strips that are sewn together to create a block.

Strip 1
Cast on 23 sts using US 5 (3.75mm/no.9) needles and yarn A. Beg with a RS row and row 1 of the chart, work until 116 rows completed.
Bind (cast) off sts.

Strip 2
Cast on 23 sts using US 5 (3.75mm/no.9) needles and yarn E. Beg with a RS row and row 1 of the chart, work until 116 rows completed.
Bind (cast) off sts.

Strip 3
Cast on 23 sts using US 5 (3.75mm/no.9) needles and yarn D. Beg with a RS row and row 1 of the chart, work until 116 rows completed.
Bind (cast) off sts.

Strip 4
Cast on 23 sts using US 5 (3.75mm/no.9) needles and yarn B. Beg with a RS row and row 1 of the chart, work until 116 rows completed.
Bind (cast) off sts.

Darn in ends on the WS of the 4 strips.
With WS facing and using a damp pressing cloth and a moderate iron lightly press the strips.
Sew them together as folls to create a single block:
Strip 1 to strip 2.
Strip 2 to strip 3.
Strip 3 to strip 4.

Key

- ☐ orange (A)
- ☐ aqua (B)
- ■ pink (C)
- ☐ yellow (D)
- ■ purple (E)
- ☐ green (F)
- ☐ K on RS, P on WS

Buttonhole Panel

With RS facing pick up and knit
87 sts along bound (cast) off edge
of front panel using US 3
(3.25mm/no.10) needles
and yarn C.

✱✱NEXT ROW (WS): Knit.
Change to US 5 (3.75mm/no.9)
needles.

Stripe patt repeat

ROW 1 (RS): Yarn F, knit.

ROW 2 (WS): Yarn F, purl.

ROWS 3–6: Rep rows 1–2 twice.
Change to US 3 (3.25mm/no.10)
needles.

ROW 7: Yarn D, knit.

ROW 8: Yarn D, knit.
Change to US 5 (3.75mm/no.9)
needles.

ROWS 9–14: Rep rows 1–6 once.
Change to US 3 (3.25mm/no.10)
needles.

ROW 15: Yarn E, knit.

ROW 16: Yarn E, knit.
Change to US 5 (3.75mm/no.9)
needles.

ROWS 17–22: Rep rows 1–6 once.
Change to US 3 (3.25mm/no.10)
needles.

ROW 23: Yarn A, knit.

ROW 24: Yarn A, knit.
Change to US 5 (3.75mm/no.9)
needles.

ROWS 25–30: Rep rows 1–6 once.

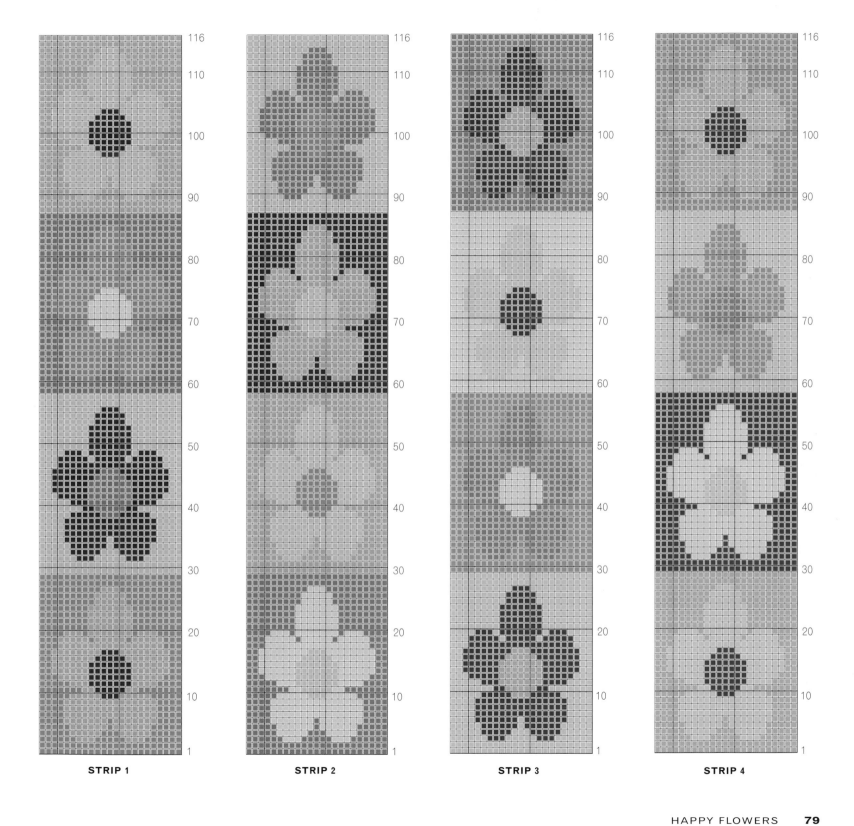

STRIP 1 STRIP 2 STRIP 3 STRIP 4

Change to US 3 (3.25mm/no.10) needles.

ROW 31: Yarn B, knit.

ROW 32: Yarn B, knit.

Change to US 5 (3.75mm/no.9) needles.

ROWS 33–38: Rep rows 1–6 once.

Change to US 3 (3.25mm/no.10) needles.

ROW 39: Yarn C, knit.

ROW 40: Yarn C, knit.

Change to US 5 (3.75mm/no.9) needles.

ROWS 41–54: Rep rows 1–14.✷✷

Buttonhole band

Change to US 3 (3.25mm/no.10) needles.

NEXT ROW (RS): Yarn E, knit.

NEXT ROW (WS): Yarn E, knit.

NEXT ROW: Yarn A, knit.

NEXT ROW: Yarn A, knit.

NEXT ROW: Yarn B, knit.

NEXT ROW: Yarn B, knit.

NEXT ROW (RS) (BUTTONHOLE ROW): Yarn C, K4, [bind (cast) off next 3 sts, K16 including st already on the needle] four times, bind (cast) off next 3 sts, K4 including st already on the needle.

NEXT ROW (WS): Yarn C, K4, [turn work (RS facing), cast on 3 sts, turn work again (WS facing), K16] four times, turn work (RS facing), cast on 3 sts, turn work again (WS facing), K4.

NEXT ROW: Yarn D, knit.

NEXT ROW: Yarn D, knit.

NEXT ROW: Yarn E, knit.

With WS facing, bind (cast) off sts knitwise using yarn E.

Buttonband Panel

With RS facing pick up and knit 87 sts along cast on edge of front panel using US 3 (3.25mm/no.10) needles and yarn C.

Rep instructions for buttonhole panel from ✷✷ to ✷✷, but use yarn A in place of yarn F and yarn F in place of yarn A.

Buttonband

Change to US 3 (3.25mm/no.10) needles.

Beg with a RS row, cont in stockinette (stocking) stitch for 16 rows using yarn C.

Bind (cast) off sts knitwise.

FINISHING

Darn in ends on the WS of the work. With WS facing and using a moderate iron and a damp pressing cloth, lightly press cushion cover.

Mark the center point along the side seam edges of front panel.

Sew side seams of buttonhole panel to front panel ensuring that buttonholes are in line with the marked center point.

Sew side seams of buttonband panel to front panel, inserting broad stockinette (stocking) stitch border at finished edge under the finished edge of the buttonhole panel, and sew down into place.

Sew buttons onto buttonband to correspond with buttonholes.

English garden

Rosebud pillow

A crisp checkerboard pattern embroidered with small rosebuds in fresh pastel shades provides the basis for this pillow. There are two versions of the design offered here—one in sweet lilac, embellished with shell buttons and beads and fastened across the top with beaded ties, and the other in a spring green colorway with a decorative rose button fastening. If you enjoy knitting these pillows, consider making the bolster on page 86 to complement them.

SIZE
14in × 18in (35cm × 45cm)

MATERIALS
1 pair US 5 (3.75mm/no.9) needles
1 pair US 2/3 (3mm/no.11) needles

Colorway 1 (main picture front)
Yarn
Rowan Handknit DK Cotton
1¾oz (50g) balls

light green (A)	8
gray/blue (B)	1
pale pink (C)	1
magenta (D)	small amount

Buttons
Edwardian rose ceramic	6

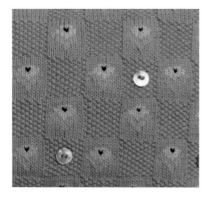

Colorway 2 (main picture back)
Yarn
Rowan Handknit DK Cotton
1¾oz (50g) balls

lilac (A)	8
green (B)	1
pale pink (C)	1
magenta (D)	small amount

Beads
⅛in (3mm) pebble beads
purple	236

Buttons
shell	10

GAUGE (TENSION)
22 sts and 30 rows to 4in (10cm) measured over stockinette (stocking) stitch using US 5 (3.75mm/no.9) needles.

ABBREVIATIONS
See page 127.

TECHNIQUES
Adding embroidery to knitting, see page 124.
Knitting with beads, see page 120.
Buttonholes, see page 123.
Darning in ends, see page 120.
Blocking and pressing, see page 124.
Sewing up, see page 125.

KNIT
Front Panel
Cast on 101 sts using US 5 (3.75mm/no.9) needles and yarn A.
30-row seed (moss) stitch patt repeat
ROW 1 (RS): K10, [(P1, K1) four times, P1, K9] five times, K1.
ROW 2 (WS): K1, P9 [(P1, K1) four times, P10] five times, K1.
ROWS 3–14: Rep rows 1–2 six times.
ROW 15: As row 1.
ROW 16 (WS): K2, [P1, K1] four times, [P9, (K1, P1) four times, K1] five times, K1.
ROW 17 (RS): K2, [P1, K1] four times, [K9, (K1, P1) four times, K1] five times, K1.
ROWS 18–29: Rep rows 16–17 six times.
ROW 30: As row 16.

Colorway 1
Rep the 30-row patt repeat three times in total. Rep patt repeat rows 1–15.
(105 rows)
Buttonhole band
Change to US 2/3 (3mm/no.11) needles. Rep patt repeat rows 16–22.
(112 rows)
NEXT ROW (RS) (BUTTONHOLE ROW): K2, P1, K1 [bind (cast) off next 3 sts, K1, P1, K11, P1, K1 including st already on the needle] five

times, bind (cast) off 3 sts, K1, P1, K2 including st already on needle.
NEXT ROW (WS): K2, P1, K1 [turn work (RS facing), cast on 3 sts, turn work again (WS facing), K1, P1, K1, P9, K1, P1, K1] five times, turn work (RS facing), cast on 3 sts, turn work again (WS facing), K1, P1, K2.
Rep patt repeat rows 25–28.
NEXT ROW (RS): K2, [P1, K1] to last st, K1.
With WS facing bind (cast) off sts knitwise.

Colorway 2
Rep the 30-row patt repeat three times in total. Rep patt repeat rows 1–15. Mark the last row at each side edge with a piece of thread. *(105 rows)*
**Front band (with ties)
Change to US 2/3 (3mm/no.11) needles. Rep patt repeat rows 16–30.
NEXT ROW (RS): Knit.
NEXT ROW (WS): Knit (to form a fold line for the buttonband).
Beg with a k row, work 13 rows in stockinette (stocking) stitch,

ending with a RS row.
Leave sts on needle.
Binding (casting) off buttonband
With WS facing and using a US 2/3 (3mm/no.11) needle, pick up all of the stitches across the WS of the knitting, following the row marked earlier on. When the stitches are picked up the knitting needle should be parallel with the needle that is holding the stitches from the buttonband. Using a US 5 (3.75mm/no.9) needle bind (cast) off the stitches together.**

Back Panel
Both colorways
With RS facing and using a US 2/3 (3.00mm/no.11) needle and yarn A, pick up and knit 101 sts along the cast on edge of the front panel.
NEXT ROW (WS): Knit.
Change to US 5 (3.75mm/no.9) needles.
NEXT ROW (RS): Knit.
Beg with a WS row, work rows

16–30 of the seed (moss) stitch patt repeat.
Rep patt repeat rows 1–30, 3 times more ending with a WS row.
Mark the last row at each side edge with a piece of thread.
Rep patt repeat rows 1–14 once more ending with a WS row.
Rep instructions for knitting and binding (casting) off front band with ties (front panel, colorway 2) from ** to **.

EMBELLISHING
Both colorways
Swiss darn rosebuds onto the stockinette (stocking) stitch squares on front panel, following chart and using photograph for guidance.

Colorway 2
Sew shell buttons and beads (2 for each button) onto seed (moss) stitch squares on front panel, using photograph for guidance.

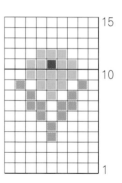

EMBROIDERED ROSEBUD

Key
☐ lilac or light green (A)

▩ green or gray/blue (B)

☐ pale pink (C)

■ magenta (D)

FINISHING
Darn in ends on the WS of the work. With WS facing and using a damp pressing cloth and a moderate iron, lightly press the cushion cover.

Sew side seams together (including the buttonhole band and buttonband at the top).

Colorway 1
Sew buttons onto buttonband to correspond with buttonholes.

Colorway 2
Knitted ties
(6 on front panel, 6 on back panel.) Thread 216 beads onto the yarn. Using US 2/3 (3mm/no.11) needles and with RS facing, pick up and knit 3 sts from the top edge of the middle of the first seed (moss) stitch square on the front panel.
NEXT ROW (WS): **K1, P1, K1.**
NEXT ROW (RS): **K1, pb, K1.**
Rep the last two rows until 18 beads have been knitted in. Bind (cast) off sts.
Make 6 ties in this way, picking up from each seed (moss) st square. Rep for ties on back panel, but pick up and knit sts from the top edge of the middle of the stockinette (stocking) stitch squares on the back panel.

Cable and rosebud bolster

Ribbed cables, seed (moss) stitch patterns and slipped stitches are combined to create an embossed effect. The stitch definition is enhanced by the soft, stretchy cotton yarn that has been used to knit up this design. The addition of delicately colored rosebuds embroidered onto the knitting softens the regimented pattern repeat and adds extra interest. The bolster ends are intriguing to knit, using the technique of short-row shaping to make circular panels.

SIZE

18in × 7in (45cm × 17cm) bolster

MATERIALS

1 pair US 5 (3.75mm/no.9) needles
1 pair US 7 (4.5mm/no.7) needles
Cable needle

Yarn

Rowan Calmer
1¾oz (50g) balls

pale blue (A)	5
green (B)	1
pale pink (C)	1
magenta (D)	small amount

Buttons

Edwardian rose ceramic   6

GAUGE (TENSION)

22 sts and 30 rows to 4in (10cm) measured over stockinette (stocking) stitch using US 7 (4.5mm/no.7) needles.

ABBREVIATIONS

Wrap st = **slip st, yf between needles, slip st back onto left-hand needle, yb.**
c8b = **cable 8 back: slip next 4 sts onto cable needle and hold at back of work, K4, then K4 sts from the cable needle**
See also page 127.

TECHNIQUES

Cables, see page 122.
Buttonholes, see page 123.
Short-row shaping, page 122.
Embroidery, page 124.
Blocking and pressing,
    see page 124.
Sewing up, see page 125.

KNIT
Main Panel

Cast on 105 sts using US 7 (4.5mm/no.7) needles.
Buttonband
Work 11 rows in stockinette (stocking) stitch, ending with a RS row.
Setting the sts and increasing for the cable patt
NEXT ROW (WS): **K1, P1, [K1, P4, K1, P2, K1, P7, K1, P2] five times, K1, P4, K1, P1, K1.**
NEXT ROW (INC) (RS): **K1, sl1 purlwise, [P1, inc once into each of the next 4 sts, P1, yb, sl1 purlwise, P1, K9, P1, yb, sl1 purlwise, yf] five times, P1, inc once into each of the next 4 sts, P1, yb, sl1 purlwise, K1.**
(129 sts)
NEXT ROW (WS): **K1, P1, [K1, P8, K1, P2, K1, P3, K1, P3, K1, P2] five times, K1, P8, K1, P1, K1.**
Cable patt repeat
ROW 1 (RS): **K1, sl1 purlwise, yf, [P1, K8, P1, yb, sl1 purlwise, yf, P1, K9, P1, yb, sl1 purlwise, yf] five times, P1, K8, P1, yb, sl1 purlwise, K1.**

ROW 2 (WS): **K1, P1, [K1, P8, (K1, P2) twice, K1, P1, (K1, P2) twice] five times, K1, P8, K1, P1, K1.**
ROW 3: **As row 1.**
ROW 4: **K1, P1, [K1, P8, K1, P2, (K1, P1) four times, K1, P2] five times, K1, P8, K1, P1, K1.**
ROW 5: **As row 1.**
ROW 6: **As row 2.**
ROW 7: **As row 1.**
ROW 8: **K1, P1, [K1, P8, K1, P2, K1, P3, K1, P3, K1, P2] five times, K1, P8, K1, P1, K1.**
ROW 9: **K1, sl1 purlwise, yf, [P1, c8b, P1, yb, sl1 purlwise, yf, P1, K9, P1, yb, sl1 purlwise, yf] five times, P1, c8b, P1, yb, sl1 purlwise, K1.**
ROW 10: **K1, P1, [(K1, P1) twice, K2, (P1, K1) twice, P2, K1, P7, K1, P2] five times, [K1, P1] twice, K2, [P1, K1] three times.**
ROW 11: **K1, sl1 purlwise, yf, [(P1, K1) twice, P2, (K1, P1) twice, yb, sl1 purlwise, yf, P1, K9, P1, yb, sl1 purlwise, yf] five times, [P1, K1] twice, P2, K1, P1, K1, P1, yb, sl1 purlwise, K1.**
ROWS 12–23: **Rep rows 10–11 six times more.**
ROW 24: **As row 10.**
ROW 25: **As row 9.**
ROW 26: **As row 8.**
ROWS 27–34: **Rep rows 1–8.**
Rep rows 9–34 seven times more.
Buttonhole band
Change to US 5 (3.75mm/no.9) needles.
NEXT ROW (RS) (DEC): **K1, sl1 purlwise,**

yf, [P1, K2tog four times, P1, yb, sl1 purlwise, yf, P1, K9, P1, yb, sl1 purlwise, yf] five times, P1, K2tog four times, P1, yb, sl1 purlwise, K1.
(105 sts)
NEXT ROW (WS) (INC): **P52, inc once into next st, P52.**
(106 sts)
NEXT ROW (RS): **[K1, P1] to end.**
NEXT ROW (WS): **[P1, K1] to end.**
Rep the last 2 rows once more.
NEXT ROW (RS) (BUTTONHOLE ROW):
[K1, P1] twice, [bind (cast) off next 3 sts, (P1, K1) eight times including st already on needle, bind (cast) off next 3 sts, (K1, P1) eight times including st already on needle] twice, bind (cast) off next 3 sts, [P1, K1] eight times including st already on needle, bind (cast) off next 3 sts, [K1, P1] twice including st already on needle.
NEXT ROW (WS): **[P1, K1] twice, [turn work (RS facing) cast on 3 sts, turn work again (WS facing), (K1, P1) eight times, turn work (RS facing), cast on 3 sts, turn work again (WS facing), (P1, K1) eight times] twice, turn work (RS facing), cast on 3 sts, turn work again (WS facing), [K1, P1] eight times, turn work (RS facing), cast on 3 sts, turn work again (WS facing), [P1, K1] twice.**
NEXT ROW (RS): **[K1, P1] to end.**
NEXT ROW (WS): **[P1, K1] to end.**
NEXT ROW (RS): **[K1, P1] to end.**
With WS facing bind (cast) off sts knitwise.

End Circular Panels

(make 2)

Cast on 24 sts using US 5 (3.75mm/no.9) needles and yarn A.

12-row patt repeat

ROW 1 (RS): Knit to last 4 sts, wrap st, turn.

ROW 2 (WS): Purl to end of row.

ROW 3: Knit to last 8 sts, wrap st, turn.

ROW 4: Purl to end of row.

ROW 5: Knit to last 12 sts, wrap st, turn.

ROW 6: Purl to end of row.

ROW 7: Knit to last 16 sts, wrap st, turn.

ROW 8: Purl to end of row.

ROW 9: Knit to last 20 sts, wrap st, turn.

ROW 10: Purl to end of row.

ROW 11: Knit.

ROW 12: Knit.

Rep the 12-row patt repeat sixteen times in total.

Bind (cast) off sts.

Sew bound (cast) off edge to cast on edge to create a circular panel.

EMBELLISHING

Swiss darn rosebuds onto main panel, positioning them as indicated on the chart, onto the panel in between the cable stitch panels, positioned between the textured diamonds.

Note: The center stitch of row 26 will be obscured by the reverse stockinette (stocking) stitch on row 27.

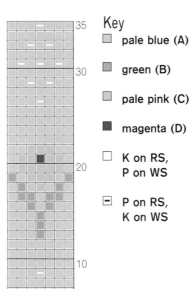

EMBROIDERED ROSEBUD

Key

☐ pale blue (A)

▨ green (B)

▤ pale pink (C)

■ magenta (D)

☐ K on RS, P on WS

⊟ P on RS, K on WS

FINISHING

Darn in ends on the WS of the work. With WS facing and using a damp pressing cloth and a cool iron, lightly press the main panel. Wrap the main panel around the bolster.

Insert the broad stockinette (stocking) stitch button band under the finished edge of the buttonhole band and sew down into place.

Sew buttons onto buttonband to correspond with buttonholes.

Sew circular panels onto each end, easing them into place.

Dewdrop

There is something quite magical about walking through a grassy field in the early morning and seeing the plants encrusted with millions of glistening dewdrops. Here, tiny silver beads are knitted into an all-over lace pattern to create a pretty and delicate fabric that simulates this natural phenomenon.

SIZE
16in × 16in (40cm × 40cm)

MATERIALS
1 pair US 2/3 (3mm/no.11) needles
1 pair US 1 (2.25mm/no.13) needles

Yarn
Rowan 4–ply Cotton
1¾oz (50g) balls
    pale green   5

Beads
    silver   2800 approx.

GAUGE (TENSION)
28 sts and 38 rows to 4in (10cm) measured over stockinette (stocking) stitch using US 2/3 (3mm/no.11) needles.

ABBREVIATIONS
See page 127.

TECHNIQUES
Knitting with beads, see page 120.
Blocking and pressing,
   see page 124.
Sewing up, see page 125.

KNIT
Front Panel
Thread approximately 400 beads onto yarn. When you run out of beads break yarn at end of row, thread on 400 more beads and rejoin yarn.

Cast on 113 sts using US 2/3 (3mm/no.11) needles.
NEXT ROW (WS): **Purl.**
10-row lace and bead patt repeat
ROW 1 (RS): **K6, [pb, K2tog, K2, yfon, K1, yfon, K2, sl1, K1, psso, pb, K7] five times, pb, K2tog, K2, yfon, K1, yfon, K2, sl1, K1, psso, pb, K6.**
ROWS 2, 4 AND 6 (WS): **Purl.**
ROW 3: **K5, [pb, K2tog, K2, yfon, K3, yfon, K2, sl1, K1, psso, pb, K5] five times, pb, K2tog, K2, yfon, K3, yfon, K2, sl1, K1, psso, pb, K5.**
ROW 5: **K4, [pb, K2tog, K2, yfon, K5, yfon, K2, sl1, K1, psso, pb, K3] five times, pb, K2tog, K2, yfon, K5, yfon, K2, sl1, K1, psso, pb, K4.**
ROW 7: **K3, [pb, K2tog, K2, yfon, K2, P3, K2, yfon, K2, sl1, K1, psso, pb, K1] five times, pb, K2tog, K2, yfon, K2, P3, K2, yfon, K2, sl1, K1, psso, pb, K3.**
ROW 8 (WS): **P3, [P7, K3, P8] five times, P7, K3, P10.**
ROW 9: **K2, [pb, K2tog, K2, yfon, K3, P3, K3, yfon, K2, sl1, K1, psso] five times, pb, K2tog, K2, yfon, K3, P3, K3, yfon, K2, sl1, K1, psso, pb, K2.**
ROW 10: **Purl.**
Rep the 10-row patt repeat sixteen times or until panel is square, ending with a WS row and row 10 of the patt repeat.
✳✳Top Edging
NEXT ROW (RS): **K2, [pb, K1] fifty-five times, K1.**
NEXT ROW: **Purl.**
NEXT ROW: **K3, [pb, K1] fifty-four times, K2.**

NEXT ROW: **Purl.**
NEXT ROW: **K2, [pb, K1] fifty-five times, K1.**
NEXT ROW: **Purl.**
NEXT ROW: **K3, [pb, K1] fifty-four times, K2.**
With WS facing, bind (cast) off sts knitwise.
Mark with colored thread the 6 groups of 3 reverse stockinette (stocking) sts (P3) on row 9 of the last block of the pattern (you will pick up these groups of sts later to knit the beaded ties) **✳✳**.

Back Panel
Thread beads onto yarn.
With RS facing and using US 1 (2.25mm/no.13) needles, pick up and knit 113 sts along the cast on edge of the front panel.
NEXT ROW (WS): **Knit.**
NEXT ROW (RS): **Purl.**
NEXT ROW (WS): **Purl.**
Change to US 2/3 (3mm/no.11) needles.
2-row beaded patt repeat
ROW 1 (RS): **K2, [pb, K8] twelve times, pb, K2.**
ROW 2 (WS): **Purl.**
Rep the 2-row beaded patt repeat until work matches front panel to beg of top edging.
Rep instructions for front panel from **✳✳** to **✳✳**.

FINISHING
With WS facing and using a damp pressing cloth and a moderate iron, lightly press the cushion cover.
Sew side seams together.

Knitted ties
6 on each panel
Knit 12 beaded ties as folls:
Thread beads onto yarn.
With RS facing and using US 1 (2.25mm/no.13) needles, pick up and knit one set of the 3 marked reverse stockinette (stocking) sts.
2-row beaded patt repeat
ROW 1 (WS): **K1, P1, K1.**
ROW 2 (RS): **K1, pb, K1.**
Rep the 2 row beaded patt repeat until tie measures 6in (15cm).
Bind (cast) off sts.
Sew in ends.
Rep with the other 11 sets of marked sts.

Flora

The colors and floral motifs in this design were inspired by a rambling rose quilt cover print. I have simplified the shapes of the roses and rosebuds and linked them together to create a decorative pattern that is repeated across the front panel. The bead and lace stitch pattern between the rose panels and on the back panels add to the elegance of this stylish design.

SIZE
14in × 14in (35cm × 35cm)

MATERIALS
1 pair US 2/3 (3mm/no.11) needles
1 pair US 2 (2.75mm/no.12) needles

Yarn
Rowan Glace Cotton
1¾oz (50g) balls

yellow (A)	2
magenta (B)	1
bright pink (C)	1
purple (D)	1
palest pink (E)	1
green (F)	1
mid pink (G)	3

Beads
⅛in (3mm) pebble beads
pale pink   1,250 approx.

Buttons
Edwardian rose ceramic   5

GAUGE (TENSION)
25 sts and 34 rows to 4in (10cm) measured over stockinette (stocking) stitch using US 2/3 (3mm/no.11) needles.

ABBREVIATIONS
See page 127.

TECHNIQUES
Knitting with beads, see page 120.
Intarsia knitting, see page 119.
Buttonholes, see page 123.
Blocking and pressing,
    see page 124.
Sewing up, see page 125.
Note: As an alternative to knitting in all of the colors, the rosehead and rosebud can be knitted in blocks, using yarn C and yarn F respectively. The other colors can then be Swiss darned onto the front panel after knitting.

KNIT
Front Panel
Cast on 97 sts using US 2/3 (3mm/no.11) needles and yarn A. Beg with a RS row and starting with row 1 of the chart and using the intarsia technique, work until chart row 88 completed.
Rep chart rows 23–55 once more.
Rep chart rows 2–9 once more
Yarn A purl 1 row.
(130 rows in total)
Bind (cast) off sts.
Mark the center point along side edges of front panel.

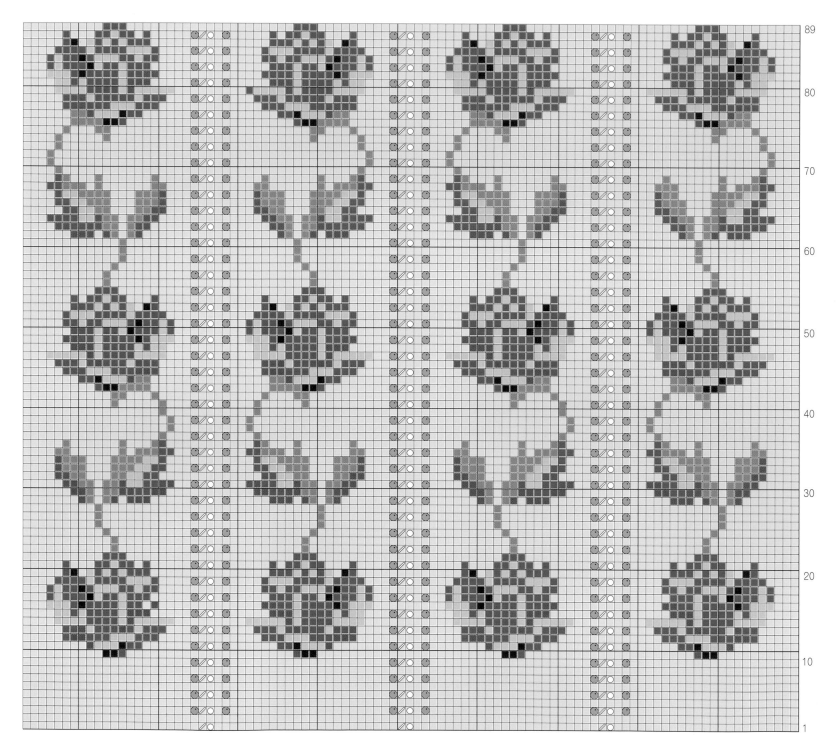

FLORA FRONT PANEL CHART

Key

- ☐ yellow (A)
- ◉ pink bead
- ■ magenta (B)
- ■ bright pink (C)
- ▥ purple (D)
- ☐ palest pink (E)
- ▨ green (F)
- ☐ K on RS, P on WS
- ◉ yarn forward
- ▨ k2tog

Buttonhole Panel

Thread beads onto yarn G.
With RS facing and using a US 2 (2.75mm/no.12) needle and yarn F, pick up and knit 97 sts along the bound (cast) off edge of the front panel.
NEXT ROW (WS): Knit.
** Change to US 2/3 (3mm/no.11) needles.
Cont to work buttonhole panel in yarn G only.
NEXT ROW (RS): Knit.
NEXT ROW (DEC) (WS): P10, P2tog, [P23, P2tog] three times, P10.
(93 sts)
2-row bead and lace stitch patt repeat
ROW 1 (RS): K3, [P1, K1, P1, K2, pb, K1, yfon, K2tog, pb, K2] seven times, P1, K1, P1, K3.
ROW 2 (WS): P3, [P1, K1, P10] seven times, P1, K1, P4.
Beg with a RS row, rep the 2-row bead and lace stitch patt rep until work is 5 rows shorter than to

marked center points along side edges of front panel, ending with a RS row.**
NEXT ROW (INC) (WS): P10, inc once into the next st, [P23, inc once into the next st] three times, P10.
(97 sts)
Buttonhole band
Change to US 2 (2.75mm/no.12) needles.
NEXT ROW (RS): Knit.
NEXT ROW (WS): Purl.
Rep the last 2 rows once more.
NEXT ROW (RS) (BUTTONHOLE ROW): K5, [bind (cast) off next 3 sts, K18 including st already on the needle] four times, bind (cast) off next 3 sts, K5 including st already on needle.

NEXT ROW (WS): P5, [turn work (RS facing), cast on 3 sts, turn work again (WS facing), P18] four times, turn work (RS facing), cast on 3 sts, turn work again (WS facing), P5.
NEXT ROW (RS): Knit.
NEXT ROW (WS): Purl.
NEXT ROW (RS): Knit.
NEXT ROW (WS): [K1, P1] to last st, K1.
NEXT ROW (RS): [K1, P1] to last st, K1.
With WS facing, bind (cast) off sts knitwise.

Buttonband Panel

Thread beads onto yarn G.
With RS facing and using a US 2 (2.75mm/no.12) needle and yarn F, pick up and knit 97 sts along the cast on edge of the front panel.
NEXT ROW (WS): Knit.
Rep patt instructions for buttonhole panel from ** to **.
Buttonband
Change to US 2 (2.75mm/no.12) needles.
Rep the 2-row bead and lace stitch patt repeat four times more.
NEXT ROW (INC) (WS): P10, inc once into the next st, [P23, inc once into the next st] three times, P10.
(97 sts)
NEXT ROW (RS): Knit.
NEXT ROW (WS): Purl.
Rep the last 2 rows seven times more.
Bind (cast off) sts.

FINISHING

Darn in ends on the WS of the work. With WS facing and using a damp pressing cloth and a moderate iron, lightly press the cushion cover.

Sew side seams of buttonhole panel to front panel ensuring that buttonholes are in line with the marked center point.

Sew side seams of buttonband panel to front panel, inserting broad stockinette (stocking) stitch border at finished edge under the finished edge of the buttonhole panel, and sew down into place.

Turn cover inside out and press seams.

Sew buttons onto buttonband to correspond with buttonholes.

Cupcake

When I was growing up as a child my mother used to treat us at the weekends to freshly baked cakes from the local bakery shop. It was a real old-fashioned cake shop that sold everything from crisp white wedding cakes to buns dipped in pretty pastel-colored icing. In this cushion cover design concentric squares in soft fondant shades are laced with beads and embellished with delicate shell buttons, echoing the charm of these mouth-watering treats.

SIZE

15in × 15in (38cm × 38cm)

MATERIALS

1 pair US 2/3 (3mm/no.11) needles
1 pair US 2 (2.75mm/no.12) needles

Colorway 1 (main picture)

Yarn

Rowan Glace Cotton
1¾oz (50g) balls

light beige (A)	3
cream (B)	3

Beads

⅛in (3mm) pebble beads

silver	950 approx.

Buttons

large shell	5
small shell	113

Colorway 2

Yarn

Rowan Glace Cotton
1¾oz (50g) balls

pink (A)	3
cream (B)	3

Beads

⅛in (3mm) pebble beads

pale pink	950 approx.

Buttons

large shell	5
small shell	113

GAUGE (TENSION)

25 sts and 34 rows to 4in (10cm) measured over stockinette (stocking) stitch using US 2/3 (3mm/no.11) needles.

ABBREVIATIONS

See page 127.

TECHNIQUES

Knitting with beads, see page 120.
Intarsia knitting, see page 119.
Buttonholes, see page 123.
Darning in ends, see page 120.
Blocking and pressing,
    see page 124.
Sewing up, see page 125.

KNIT

Front Panel

Thread beads onto yarn A.
Cast on 97 sts using US 2/3 (3mm/no.11) needles and yarn A.
Beg with a RS row and starting with row 1 of chart and using the intarsia technique, work until chart row 143 completed, ending with a RS row.
Bind (cast) off sts.

Key

■ light beige (A)

◉ silver bead

□ cream (B)

□ K on RS, P on WS

⊟ P on RS, K on WS

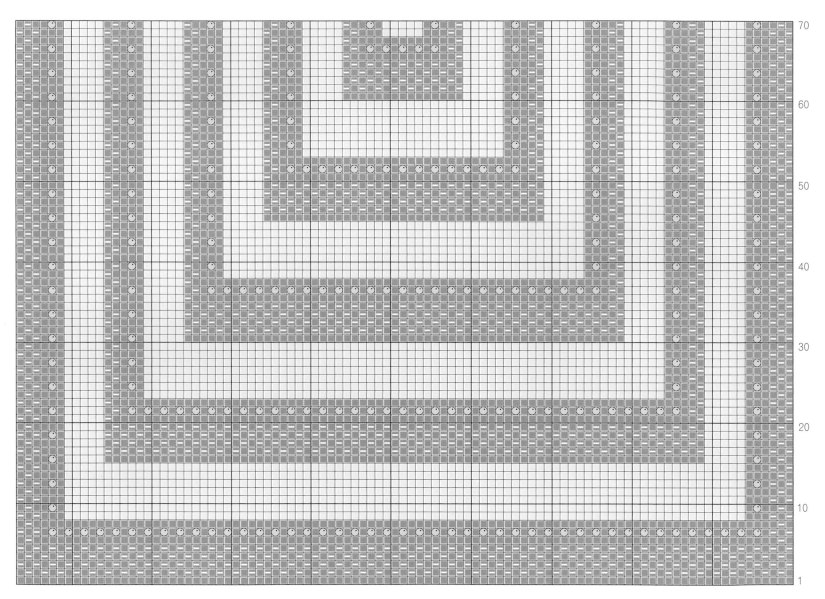

START OF CUPCAKE FRONT PANEL CHART

Key

■ light beige (A)

☐ K on RS, P on WS

⊙ silver bead

⊟ P on RS, K on WS

☐ cream (B)

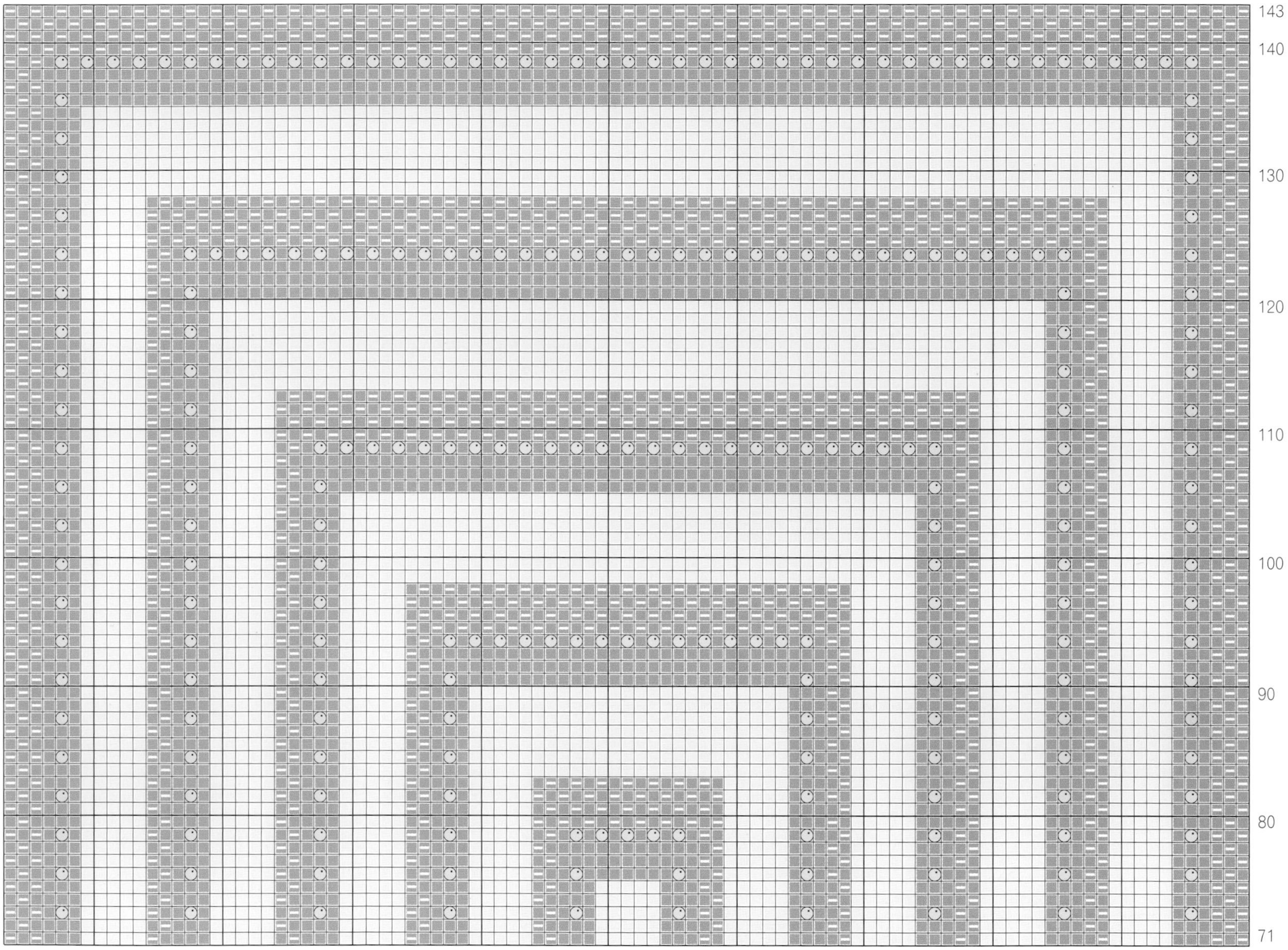

CUPCAKE FRONT PANEL CHART CONTINUED

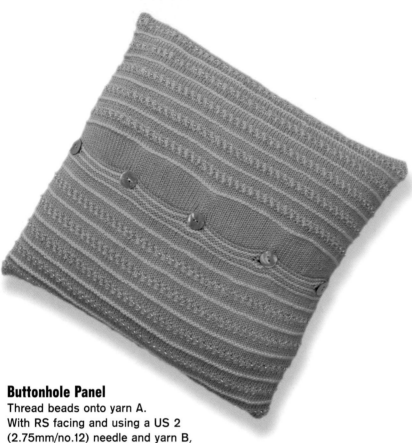

Buttonhole Panel

Thread beads onto yarn A.
With RS facing and using a US 2 (2.75mm/no.12) needle and yarn B, pick up and knit 97 sts along the bound (cast) off edge of the front panel.

** NEXT ROW (WS): **Knit.**
Change to US 2/3 (3mm/no.11) needles.

12-row bead and purl stitch patt repeat
ROW 1 (RS): **Yarn A, knit.**
ROW 2 (WS): **Yarn A, purl.**
ROWS 3–4: **Rep rows 1–2.**
ROW 5: **Yarn B, K1, [P1, yb, sl1 purlwise, yf] forty-seven times, P1, K1.**
ROW 6: **Yarn B, purl.**
ROW 7: **Yarn A, K1, [K1, pb] forty-seven times, K2.**
ROW 8: **Yarn A, K1, [K1, P1] forty-seven times, K2.**
ROWS 9–10: **Rep rows 1–2.**
ROW 11: **Yarn B, knit.**
ROW 12: **Yarn B, knit.**
Rep the 12-row patt repeat five times in total.
Rep rows 1–4 once more, ending with a WS row.
*(64 rows)***

Buttonhole band
Change to US 2 (2.75mm/no.12) needles.
Yarn B, knit 2 rows.
Yarn A, knit 2 rows.
Yarn B, knit 2 rows.
NEXT ROW (RS) (BUTTONHOLE ROW):
Yarn A, K5, [bind (cast) off next 3 sts, K18 including stitch already on needle] four times, bind (cast) off next 3 sts, K5 including stitch already on needle.
NEXT ROW (WS): **Yarn A, K5, [turn work (RS facing), cast on 3 sts, turn work again (WS facing), K18] four times, turn work (RS facing), cast on 3 sts, turn work again (WS facing), K5.**
Yarn B, knit 2 rows.
Yarn A, knit 1 row.
With WS facing and using yarn A, bind (cast) off sts knitwise.

Buttonband Panel

Thread beads onto yarn A.
With RS facing and using a US 2 (2.75mm/no.12) needle and yarn B, pick up and knit 97 sts along the cast on edge of the front panel.
Rep instructions for buttonhole panel from ** to **.

Buttonband
Change to US 2 (2.75mm/no.12) needles.
Cont in yarn A only, work a further 20 rows in stockinette (stocking) stitch.
With RS facing, bind (cast) off sts knitwise.

FINISHING

Darn in ends on the WS of the work. With WS facing and using a damp pressing cloth and a moderate iron, lightly press the cushion cover.

Sew small shell buttons onto the sections of the front panel in yarn B, following the position guide below

Mark the center point along side seam edges of front panel.

Sew side seams of buttonhole panel to front panel ensuring that buttonholes are in line with the marked center point.

Sew side seams of buttonband panel to front panel, inserting the broad stockinette (stocking) stitch border at finished edge under the finished edge of the buttonhole panel, and sew down into place.

Turn cover inside out and press seams.

Sew large shell buttons onto buttonband to correspond with buttonholes.

POSITION GUIDE FOR SMALL BUTTONS

Modern minimal

Space

On a clear night I love to look up at the inky black sky and see hundreds of twinkling stars. Space is a simple design based on this experience. A smooth background is covered with self-colored beads in a repeat pattern to create a dramatic all-over design.

SIZE
16in × 16in (40cm × 40cm)

MATERIALS
1 pair US 7 (4.5mm/no.7) needles
1 pair US 5 (3.75mm/no.9) needles

Yarn
Rowan Calmer 1¾oz (50g) balls
  black   5

Beads
⅛in (4mm) pebble beads
  frosted black   655

Buttons
  circular horn   5

GAUGE (TENSION)
23 sts and 34 rows to 4in (10cm) measured over beaded stockinette (stocking) stitch using US 7 (4.5mm/no.7) needles.

ABBREVIATIONS
pb = place bead: thread beads onto yarn before starting to knit each section.
(RS): with yarn forward, slide bead up yarn, slip 1 stitch purlwise, yarn back leaving bead in front of the slipped stitch.
(WS): with yarn back, slide bead up yarn, slip 1 stitch purlwise, yarn forward leaving bead in front of slipped stitch.
See also page 127.

TECHNIQUES
Knitting with beads, see page 120.
Buttonholes, see page 123.
Blocking and pressing,
  see page 124.
Sewing up, see page 125.

KNIT
Front Panel
Cast on 89 sts using US 7 (4.5mm/no.7) needles.
Beaded patt repeat
ROW 1 (RS): Knit.
ROW 2 (WS): Purl.
ROW 3: K2, [pb, K5] fourteen times, pb, K2.
ROW 4: As row 2.
ROW 5: As row 1.
ROW 6: As row 2.
ROW 7: As row 1.
ROW 8: As row 2.
ROW 9: K5, [pb, K5] thirteen times, pb, K5.
ROW 10: As row 2.
ROW 11: As row 1.
ROW 12: As row 2.
Rep the 12-row patt repeat eleven times, then rows 1–4 once again.
(136 rows)
Bind (cast) off sts.

Buttonhole Panel
With RS facing and using US 7 (4.5mm/no.7) needles, pick up and knit 89 sts along bound (cast) off edge of front panel. Break off yarn. Slip sts back onto left-hand needle so that the RS is facing you again. Rejoin yarn.

✳✳ Rep rows 7–12 of the beaded patt repeat.
Rep rows 1–12 of the beaded patt repeat four times.
Rep rows 1–9 of the beaded patt repeat once more.
(63 rows)✳✳
Buttonhole band
Change to US 5 (3.75mm/no.9) needles.
NEXT ROW (WS): [K1, P1] to last st, K1.
NEXT ROW (RS): [K1, P1] to last st, K1. Rep the last 2 rows once more.
NEXT ROW (WS): [K1, P1] to last st, K1.
NEXT ROW (RS) (BUTTONHOLE ROW): [K1, P1] twice, K1, [bind (cast) off next 3 sts, (K1, P1) eight times including st already on needle, bind (cast) off next 3 sts, (P1, K1) eight times including st already on needle] twice, bind (cast) off next 3 sts, [K1, P1] twice, K1.
NEXT ROW (WS): [K1, P1] twice, K1, [turn work (RS facing), cast on 3 sts, turn work again (WS facing), (K1, P1) eight times, turn work (RS facing), cast on 3 sts, turn work again (WS facing), (P1, K1) eight times] twice, turn work (RS facing), cast on 3 sts, turn work again (WS facing), [K1, P1] twice, K1.
NEXT ROW (RS): [K1, P1] to last st, K1.
NEXT ROW (WS): [K1, P1] to last st, K1.
Rep the last 2 rows once more.
NEXT ROW (RS): [K1, P1] to last st, K1.
With WS facing, bind (cast) off sts knitwise.

Buttonband Panel
With RS facing and using US 7 (4.5mm/no.7) needles, pick up and knit 89 sts along cast on edge of front panel. Break off yarn.
Slip sts back onto left-hand needle so that the RS is facing you again. Rejoin yarn.
Rep instructions for buttonhole panel from ✳✳ to ✳✳.
Buttonband
Change to US 5 (3.75mm/no.9) needles.
NEXT ROW (WS): [K1, P1] to last st, K1.
NEXT ROW (RS): [K1, P1] to last st, K1.
Rep the last 2 rows eight times more.
Bind (cast) off sts.

FINISHING
With WS facing and using a damp pressing cloth and a cool iron, lightly press the cushion cover.
  Mark the center point along side seam edges of front panel.
  Sew side seams of buttonhole panel to front panel ensuring that buttonholes are in line with the marked center point.
  Sew side seams of buttonband panel to front panel, inserting broad seed (moss) stitch border at finished edge under the finished edge of the buttonhole panel, and sew down into place.
  Turn cover inside out and press seams.
  Sew buttons onto buttonband to correspond with buttonholes.

Ripple

In this design identical ribbed cables are gradually moved further apart across the knitting to simulate the gentle movement of ripples through water. The serenity of a pool or lake is reflected in this simple, measured design, which makes an easy first project for the knitter who is new to the technique of cabling.

SIZE
16in × 16in (40cm × 40cm)

MATERIALS
1 pair US 7 (4.5mm/no.7) needles
Cable needle

Yarn
Rowan Calmer 1¾oz (50g) balls
   red   4

Zip
14in (35cm) concealed zip

GAUGE (TENSION)
22 sts and 30 rows to 4in (10cm) measured over reverse stockinette (stocking) stitch using US 7 (4.5mm/no.7) needles.

ABBREVIATIONS
c10b = **slip next 5 sts onto cable needle and hold at back of work, [K1, P1] twice, K1, then K1, [P1, K1] twice from cable needle.**
Note: Knit the first and last sts of every row to create neat edges. The right-hand-edge of the front panel and the left-hand-edge of the back panel will be finished edges. See also page 127.

TECHNIQUES
Cables, see page 122.
Blocking and pressing, see page 124.
Binding (casting) off seams using three needles, see page 123.
Fitting a zip, see page 124.
Sewing up, see page 125.

KNIT
Front Panel
Cast on 92 sts using US 7 (4.5mm/no.7) needles.
NEXT ROW (WS): **K2, P5, K3, P5, K5, P5, K7, P5, K9, P5, K11, P5, K25.**
NEXT ROW (INC) (RS): **K1, P24, ✱inc once into each of the next 5 sts (making an extra 5 sts)✱, P11, rep from ✱ to ✱, P9, rep from ✱ to ✱, P7, rep from ✱ to ✱, P5, rep from ✱ to ✱, P3, rep from ✱ to ✱, P1, K1.** *(122 sts)*

NEXT ROW (WS): **K2, ✱ (P1, K1) twice, P1, (P1, K1) twice, P1✱ K3, rep from ✱ to ✱, K5, rep from ✱ to ✱, K7, rep from ✱ to ✱, K9, rep from ✱ to ✱, K11, rep from ✱ to ✱, K25.**
10-row cable patt repeat
ROW 1 (RS): **K1, P24, ✱(K1, P1) twice, K1, (K1, P1) twice, K1✱, P11, rep from ✱ to ✱, P9, rep from ✱ to ✱, P7, rep from ✱ to ✱, P5, rep from ✱ to ✱, P3, rep from ✱ to ✱, P1, K1.**
ROW 2 (WS): **K2, ✱(P1, K1) twice, P1, (P1, K1) twice, P1✱ K3, rep from ✱ to ✱, K5, rep from ✱ to ✱, K7, rep from ✱ to ✱, K9, rep from ✱ to ✱, K11, rep from ✱ to ✱, K25.**
ROW 3: **As row 1.**
ROW 4: **As row 2.**
ROW 5: **K1, P24, c10b, P11, c10b, P9, c10b, P7, c10b, P5, c10b, P3, c10b, P1, K1.**
ROW 6: **As row 2.**
ROW 7: **As row 1.**
ROW 8: **As row 2.**
ROW 9: **As row 1.**
ROW 10: **As row 2.**
Rep the 10-row patt repeat until work measures 16in (40cm) square, ending with a WS row.
NEXT ROW (RS) (DEC): **K1, P24, [K2tog] five times, P11, [K2tog] five times, P9, [K2tog] five times, P7 [K2tog] five times, P5, [K2tog] five times, P3, [K2tog] five times, P1, K1.** *(92 sts)*
Leave sts on a holder.

Back Panel

With RS facing and using US 7 (4.5mm/no.7) needles, pick up and knit 92 sts along cast on edge of front panel.

NEXT ROW (WS): K25, P5, K11, P5, K9, P5, K7, P5, K5, P5, K3, P5, K2.

NEXT ROW (RS) (INC): K1, P1, ✳ inc once into each of the next 5 sts (making an extra 5 sts),✳ P3, rep from ✳ to ✳, P5, rep from ✳ to ✳, P7, rep from ✳ to ✳, P9, rep from ✳ to ✳, P11, rep from ✳ to ✳, P24, K1. *(122 sts)*

NEXT ROW (WS): K25, ✳(P1, K1) twice, P1, (P1, K1) twice, P1✳, K11, rep from ✳ to ✳, K9, rep from ✳ to ✳, K7, rep from ✳ to ✳, K5, rep from ✳ to ✳, K3, rep from ✳ to ✳, K2.

10-row cable patt repeat

ROW 1 (RS): K1, P1, ✳(K1, P1) twice, K1, (K1, P1) twice, K1✳, P3, rep from ✳ to ✳, P5, rep from ✳ to ✳, P7, rep from ✳ to ✳, P9, rep from ✳ to ✳, P11, rep from ✳ to ✳, P24, K1.

ROW 2 (WS): K25, ✳(P1, K1) twice, P1, (P1, K1) twice, P1✳, K11, rep from ✳ to ✳, K9, rep from ✳ to ✳, K7, rep from ✳ to ✳, K5, rep from ✳ to ✳, K3, rep from ✳ to ✳, K2.

ROW 3: As row 1.

ROW 4: As row 2.

ROW 5: K1, P1, c10b, P3, c10b, P5, c10b, P7, c10b, P9, c10b, P11, c10b, P24, K1.

ROW 6: As row 2.

ROW 7: As row 1.

ROW 8: As row 2.

ROW 9: As row 1.

ROW 10: As row 2.

Rep the 10-row patt repeat until work measures 16in (40cm) square, ending with a RS row.

NEXT ROW (DEC) (RS): K1, P1, [K2tog] five times, P3, [K2tog] five times, P5, [K2tog] five times, P7, [K2tog] five times, P9, [K2tog] five times, P11, [K2tog] five times, P24, K1. *(92 sts)*

Leave sts on a holder.

FINISHING

With WS facing press the panels using a damp pressing cloth and a cool iron.

Put both sets of sts that are on holders, back onto 2 separate US 7 (4.5mm/no.7) needles.

With RS facing together and both needles pointing towards the right, bind (cast) off the sts together.

With RS facing, sew zip neatly into opening on right-hand side, ensuring that it sits centrally along this edge. Leave the ends of the work free either side of the zip. Sew these seams together after the zip is fitted, with seam on the outside of the work using a running stitch.

Sew together other side seam.

Minimal stripe

An irregular stripe pattern in soft coffee and cream shades partially covers the front panel of this cushion cover. This design is all about balance—the harmonious combination of colors and the measured spaces within which the striped and solid-colored blocks are placed. The button fastening across the back panel has been placed so that it sits in line with the start of the stripe pattern on the front panel.

SIZE
16in × 16in (40cm × 40cm)

MATERIALS
1 pair US 7 (4.5mm/no.7) needles
1 pair US 6 (4mm/no.8) needles

Yarn
Rowan Magpie Aran
3½oz (100g) hanks

brown (A)	2
mid gray (B)	1
beige (C)	1
cream (D)	small amount

Buttons
circular horn	5

GAUGE (TENSION)
19 sts and 26 rows to 4in (10cm) measured over stockinette (stocking) stitch using US 7 (4.5mm/no.7) needles.

ABBREVIATIONS
See page 127.

TECHNIQUES
Stripes using dp needles, see page 120.
Buttonholes, see page 123.
Darning in ends, see page 120.
Blocking and pressing, see page 124.
Sewing up, see page 125.

KNIT
Front Panel
Cast on 78 sts using US 7 (4.5mm/no.7) needles and yarn A. Beg with a RS row, work 64 rows in stockinette (stocking) stitch, ending with a WS row.

Stripe patt
Worked in stockinette (stocking) stitch.
ROWS 65–68: **Yarn B.**
ROWS 69–70: **Yarn A.**
ROW 71: **Yarn B.**
ROWS 72–73: **Yarn C.**
ROWS 74–79: **Yarn D.**
ROWS 80–82: **Yarn A.**
ROWS 83–84: **Yarn C.**
ROW 85: **Yarn A.**

ROWS 86–90: **Yarn B.**
ROWS 91–92: **Yarn A.**
ROWS 93–97: **Yarn C.**
ROWS 98–99: **Yarn A.**
ROW 100: **Yarn C.**
With RS facing bind (cast) off sts knitwise.

Buttonhole Panel

Yarn C only.

With RS facing pick up and knit 78 sts along bound (cast) off edge of front panel using US 6 (4mm/no.8) needles and yarn C.

NEXT ROW (WS): Knit.

Change to US 7 (4.5mm/no.7) needles.

Beg with a RS row, work in stockinette (stocking) stitch for 32 rows, ending with a WS row.

Buttonhole band

Change to US 6 (4mm/no.8) needles.

NEXT ROW (RS) (INC): [K1, P1] nineteen times, K1, m1, [K1, P1] nineteen times, K1.

(79 sts)

NEXT ROW (WS): [K1, P1] to last st, K1.

NEXT ROW (RS): [K1, P1] to last st, K1.

NEXT ROW (WS) (BUTTONHOLE ROW): [K1, P1] twice, [bind (cast) off next 3 sts, (P1, K1) seven times including st already on the needle, bind (cast) off next 3 sts, (K1, P1) seven times, including st already on the needle] twice, bind (cast) off next 3 sts, [P1, K1] twice, including st already on the needle.

NEXT ROW (RS): [K1, P1] twice, [turn work (WS facing), cast on 3 sts, turn work again (RS facing), (P1, K1) seven times including st already on the needle, turn work (WS facing), cast on 3 sts, turn work again (RS facing), (K1, P1) seven times, including st already on the needle] twice, turn work (WS facing), cast on 3 sts, turn work again (RS facing), [P1, K1] twice.

NEXT ROW (WS): [K1, P1] to last st, K1.

NEXT ROW (RS): [K1, P1] to last st, K1.

With WS facing, bind (cast) off sts knitwise.

Buttonband Panel

Worked using yarn A only.

With RS facing pick up and knit 78 sts along cast on edge of front panel using US 6 (4mm/no.8) needles.

NEXT ROW (WS): Knit.

Buttonband

Change to US 7 (4.5mm/no.7) needles.

Beg with a RS row, work in stockinette (stocking) stitch for 64 rows.

Change to US 6 (4mm/no.8) needles.

Beg with a RS row cont in stockinette (stocking) stitch for a further 10 rows.

Bind (cast) off sts knitwise.

FINISHING

Darn in ends on the WS of the work. With WS facing and using a damp pressing cloth and a moderate iron, lightly press the cushion cover.

Sew side seams of buttonhole panel to front panel ensuring that buttonholes are in line with the beginning of the stripe patt on the front panel.

Sew side seams of buttonband panel to front panel, inserting broad stockinette (stocking) stitch border at finished edge under the finished edge of the buttonhole panel, and sew down into place.

Turn cover inside out and press seams.

Sew buttons onto buttonband to correspond with buttonholes.

Target

Rows of textured circles placed in a strict, regimented pattern cover both back and front panels of this large floor cushion. I particularly like the shapes in reverse stocking stitch that are created between the circles. This large soft accessory for either the bedroom or living room adds a touch of comfort to the usually austere interior of the minimalist home.

SIZE
27in × 27in (68cm × 68cm)
(floor cushion)

MATERIALS
1 pair US 5 (3.75mm/no.9) needles
Note: A circular needle could be used if there are too many sts on the needle

Colorway 1 (main picture)
Yarn
Rowan Handknit DK Cotton
1¾oz (50g) balls
   light gray   12

Zip
22in (55cm) concealed zip

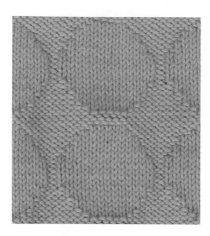

Colorway 2
Yarn
Rowan Handknit DK Cotton
1¾oz (50g) balls
   red   12

Zip
22in (55cm) concealed zip

Colorway 3
Yarn
Rowan Handknit DK Cotton
1¾oz (50g) balls
   light beige   12

Zip
22in (55cm) concealed zip

GAUGE (TENSION)
22 sts and 30 rows to 4in (10cm) measured over stockinette (stocking) stitch using US 5 (3.75mm/no.9) needles.

ABBREVIATIONS
See page 127.

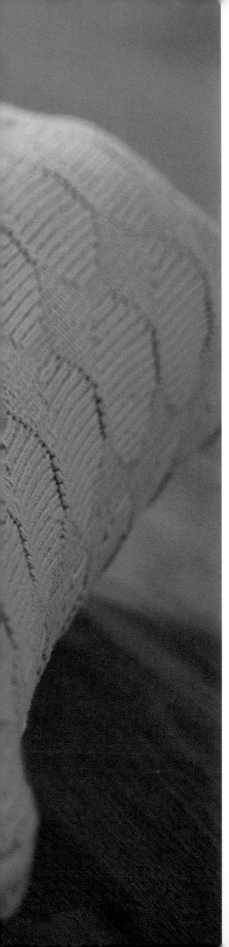

TECHNIQUES

Blocking and pressing,
  see page 124.
Fitting a zip, see page 124.
Sewing up, see page 125.

KNIT
Front Panel

Cast on 139 sts using US 5
(3.75mm/no.9) needles.
Note: Knit the first and last sts of
every row to create neat edges. The
right-hand-edge of the front panel
and the left-hand-edge of back
panel will be finished edges.
✳✳Beg with a RS row and row 1 of
the chart, work as folls:
ROW 1 (RS): K1, [P15] nine times,
P2, K1.
ROW 2 (WS): Knit.
ROW 3: K1, [P6, K5, P4] nine times,
P2, K1.
ROW 4: K3, [K3, P7, K5] nine times,
K1.
ROW 5: K1 [P4, K9, P2] nine times,
P2, K1.
ROW 6: K3, [K2, P9, K4] nine times,
K1.
Cont to work from chart, rep the
15-st patt repeat nine times across
each row as indicated on the
chart, until 22 rows completed.
Rep the 22-row patt repeat eight
times more.
(198 rows)
NEXT ROW (RS): Rep chart row 1.
NEXT ROW (WS): Knit.
Leave sts on a holder ✳✳.

Back Panel

With RS facing and using US 5
(3.75mm/no.9) needles, pick up
and knit 139 sts along cast on
edge of front panel.
Slip sts back onto left-hand needle
so that the RS is facing you again.
Rep instructions for front panel
from ✳✳ to ✳✳.

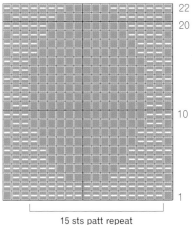

TARGET PATTERN CHART

15 sts patt repeat

22
20
10
1

Key

■ light gray

□ K on RS, P on WS

⊟ P on RS, K on WS

FINISHING

With WS facing press the panels
using a damp pressing cloth and
a moderate iron.
  Put both sets of sts that are on
holders, back onto 2 separate
US 5 (3.75mm/no.9) needles.
  With RS facing together and
both needles pointing towards the
right, bind (cast) off the sts
together using a 3rd needle.
  With front panel facing, sew zip
neatly into opening on right-hand
side, ensuring that it sits centrally
along this edge. Leave the ends of
the work free either side of the zip.
  Sew these seams together
after the zip is fitted, with seam
on the outside of the work using a
running stitch.
  Put both sets of sts that are
on holders, back onto 2 separate
US 5 (3.75mm/no.9) needles.
  With RS facing together and
both needles pointing towards the
right, bind (cast) off the sts
together using a 3rd needle.
Sew together other side seam.

Angle

Mathematics was never my strong point at school, but I did used to enjoy geometry—the study of lines and angles. A neat, precisely tesselating pattern of triangular shapes knitted in reverse and plain stockinette (stocking) stitch cover the front and back panels of this rather unusually shaped cushion cover. The side panels are knitted in reverse or plain stockinette (stocking) stitch and are sewn together to create a pill-box shape.

SIZE

10in × 35in × 3in
(25cm × 89cm × 8cm)

MATERIALS

1 circular US 5 (3.75mm/no.9)
 needle 36in (100cm)

Colorway 1 (main picture)
Yarn
Rowan Handknit DK Cotton
1¾oz (50g) balls
 light beige   11

Zip
22in (55cm) concealed zip

Colorway 2
Yarn
Rowan Handknit DK Cotton
1¾oz (50g) balls
 light gray   11

Zip
22in (55cm) concealed zip

Colorway 3
Yarn
Rowan Handknit DK Cotton
1¾oz (50g) balls
 denim blue   11

Zip
22in (55cm) concealed zip

GAUGE (TENSION)

22 sts and 30 rows to 4in (10cm)
measured over textured pattern
using US 5 (3.75mm/no.9)
needles.

ABBREVIATIONS

See page 127.

TECHNIQUES

Blocking and pressing,
 see page 124.
Fitting a zip, see page 124.
Sewing up, see page 125.

KNIT
Front Panel
Including short side panels.
Cast on 234 sts using US 5
(3.75mm/no.9) circular needle.
ROW 1 OF CHART (RS): K18, [P11]
eighteen times, P18.
ROW 2 OF CHART (WS): K18, [P1,
K10] eighteen times, P18.
Cont to work from chart for front
panel, rep the 11-st patt repeat as
indicated until chart row 22
completed.
Rep chart rows 1–22 twice more.
Rep chart rows 1–11 once more.
(77 rows)
Bind (cast) off sts.

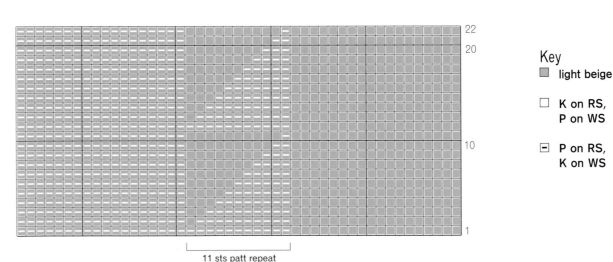

11 sts patt repeat

FRONT AND SIDE PANEL CHART

Key
- ▩ light beige
- ☐ K on RS, P on WS
- ⊟ P on RS, K on WS

Top Side Panel

With RS facing, using US 5 (3.75mm/no.9) circular needle and beginning with the 19th stitch in from the edge of the work, pick up and knit 198 sts along bound (cast) off edge of front panel.

(This should leave 18 sts not picked up at either end of the work).

Break off yarn.

Slip sts back onto left-hand needle so that the RS is facing you again. Rejoin yarn.

NEXT ROW (RS): Inc once into first st, P to last st, inc once into last st. *(200 sts)*

NEXT ROW (WS): Knit.

NEXT ROW (RS): Purl.

Rep the last 2 rows until 3in (8cm) of reverse stockinette (stocking) stitch has been worked, ending with a RS row.

With WS facing bind (cast) off sts

knitwise neatly and evenly (part of this edge will be sewn to the zip).

Bottom Side Panel

With RS facing, using US 5 (3.75mm/no.9) circular needle and beg with the 19th st in from the edge of the work, pick up and knit 198 sts along cast on edge of front panel, as for top side panel.

Break off yarn. Slip sts back onto left-hand needle so that the RS is facing you again. Rejoin yarn.

NEXT ROW (RS): Inc once into first st, K to last st, inc once into last st. *(200 sts)*

NEXT ROW (WS): Purl.

NEXT ROW (RS): Knit.

Rep the last 2 rows until 3in (8cm) in stockinette (stocking) stitch has been worked.

Bind (cast) off sts.

Back Panel

With RS facing and using US 5 (3.75mm/no.9) needles, pick up 200 sts along bound (cast) off edge of bottom side panel.

Slip sts back onto left-hand needle so that the RS is facing you again.

Beg with a RS row and starting with chart row 1 of chart for back panel, rep the 11-st patt repeat as indicated until chart row 22 completed.

Rep chart rows 1-22 twice more.

Rep chart rows 1-11 once more. *(77 rows)*

Bind (cast) off sts.

FINISHING

With WS facing and using a damp pressing cloth and a moderate iron, lightly press the cushion cover.

With RS facing sew the zip in between the bound (cast) off edge of the back panel and the bound (cast) off edge of the top side panel, ensuring that it sits centrally along this edge. Leave the ends of the work free either side of the zip. Sew these seams together after the zip is fitted, with seam on outside of work using a running stitch.

Sew together remaining seams.

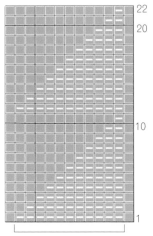

11 sts patt repeat

BACK PANEL CHART

Key

■ light beige

□ K on RS, P on WS

⊟ P on RS, K on WS

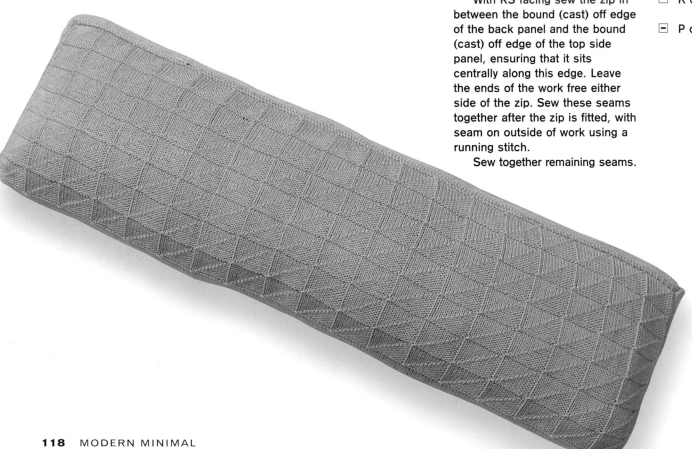

Techniques

INTARSIA KNITTING

Intarsia knitting produces a single thickness fabric that uses different balls of yarn for different areas of color. There should be very little, if any, carrying across of yarns at the back of the work.

There are several ways to help keep the separate colors of yarn organized while you are working. My preferred method is to use yarn bobbins. Small amounts of yarn can be wound onto bobbins, which should then be kept close to the back of the work while knitting, and only unwound when more yarn is needed.

Most of the intarsia patterns in this book are given in the form of a chart. It is advisable to make a color copy of the chart and to enlarge it if you prefer. This copy can be used as a worksheet on which rows can be marked off as they are worked and any notes can be made.

Joining in a new color

1 Insert the right needle into the next stitch. Place the end of the new pink yarn between the tips of the needles and across the purple yarn from left to right.

2 Take the new pink yarn under the purple yarn and knit the next stitch with it. Move the tail of pink yarn off the right needle as the new stitch is formed.

Changing colors

To avoid gaps between stitches when changing color, it is essential that the two yarns are crossed over at the back of the work.

1 On a knit row, insert the right needle into the next stitch. Place the old purple yarn over the new pink yarn. Pull the new pink yarn up and knit the stitch.

2 On a purl row, insert the right needle into the next stitch. Place the old pink yarn over the new purple yarn. Pull the new purple yarn up and purl the next stitch.

Darning in ends

When an intarsia square is completed there will be loose ends to darn in on the back of the work.

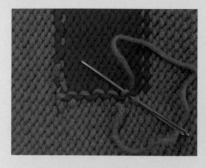

1 Darn the ends around shapes by darning through the loops of the same color in one direction first.

2 Then darn the end back on itself, stretching the work before cutting the end of the yarn.

STRIPES USING DP NEEDLES

If you are knitting a stripe pattern that has uneven rows, you can avoid breaking off the yarn and rejoining it by knitting on double-pointed or circular needles as follows.

1 If the yarn you need is at the other end of the work, push the stitches to the other end of the needle.

2 Pick up the yarn and continue, making sure that you keep in the correct pattern for the row.

KNITTING WITH BEADS

There are many different types of bead available, but not all of them are suitable for hand-knitting. When choosing beads it is important to check that the bead hole is big enough for the yarn to pass through. In addition the weight and size of the beads also needs to be considered. For example, large heavy beads on 4-ply knitting will look clumsy and cause the fabric to sag. It is also wise to check whether the beads you are using are washable, as some may not be.

When you have chosen your beads, you must thread them onto the yarn before you start to knit. There is a very easy way to do this.

Threading beads onto yarn

Place a length of sewing cotton beneath the yarn, then bring the two ends of the cotton together and thread both ends through a sewing needle. Thread the beads onto the needle, then push them down the sewing cotton and onto the knitting yarn. Remember that the first bead you thread onto the yarn will be the last one to be knitted in.

ADDING BEADS WITH A SLIP STITCH

This is my preferred method of adding beads to knitting, and it works on both wrong-side and right-side rows. The beads sit in front of a slipped stitch and hang down slightly from where they are knitted in. I have found that if the yarn is held quite firmly and the next stitch after the bead is knitted tightly, the bead sits very neatly and snugly against the knitting.

Adding beads on a right side row

1 Work to where the bead is to be placed. Bring the yarn forward between the points of the needles.

2 Push a bead up the yarn to the front of the work, so that it rests in front of the right-hand needle.

3 Slip the next stitch purlwise from the left-hand to the right-hand needle, leaving the bead in front of the slipped stitch.

4 Take the yarn between the needles to the back of the work and continue in pattern. The bead is now secured in position.

Adding beads on a wrong side row
When beads are placed on a wrong side row the instructions are almost the same.

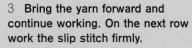

1 When a bead is to be added, take the yarn back between the needle points and push a bead up to the front of the work.

2 Slip the next stitch exactly as above.

3 Bring the yarn forward and continue working. On the next row work the slip stitch firmly.

Adding beads to reverse stockinette (stocking) stitch
The principle is the same. Place the bead with the yarn at front of work. Slide a bead up so that it rests in front of the right-hand needle. Slip the next stitch purlwise and keeping yarn at front of work pull firmly so that bead sits in front of slipped stitch then purl the next stitch.

LOOP STITCH

Loops of yarn can be knitted into a garter stitch background to create a pile fabric. A loop is made on the RS of the work as follows.

1 Knit next stitch but leave it on the left-hand needle. Bring yarn forward between needles.

2 Wrap the yarn around your thumb to make a loop.

3 Then take yarn back between the needles and knit the same stitch again, this time slipping the stitch off the left-hand needle and the loop off your thumb. This will create an extra stitch.

4 Bring yarn forward between the needles and then back over the needle to the WS of the work. This will create another extra stitch.

5 Lift the first stitch in the sequence over the last two. Then lift the second stitch in the sequence over the last one. Continue knitting until the next loop is required.

CABLES

Cables are the crossing of one set of stitches over another to create a twisted rope effect. Stitches can be crossed over at the front or the back of the work; this determines whether the cable twists to the left or to the right. Stitches held at the front of the work will twist the cable to the left, stitches held at the back of the work will twist the cable to the right. Cables are usually knitted in stockinette (stocking) stitch on a background of reverse stockinette (stocking) stitch, though a background of stockinette (stocking) stitch can also work well. Usually the number of stitches that are crossed are half of the amount stated in the abbreviation, ie: c8b means cross 4 stitches with 4 stitches. There are many different variations, so it is best to read the instructions carefully before starting to knit. This example shows how to work c8b.

c8b

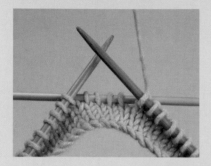

1 Slip the next 4 stitches onto the cable needle and hold at the back of the work.

2 Knit 4 stitches from the left-hand needle.

3 Then knit the 4 stitches that are on the cable needle.

Make sure that you pull the yarn firmly and knit the stitches tightly to avoid any gaps in the work.

SHORT-ROW SHAPING

Pieces of knitted fabric can be shaped by working part of the way across a row and then turning the knitting and working back along the same section – this is called short-row shaping. The frequency of the working and turning can be altered to create different shapes. It can be used to shape edges in garments or to create complete shapes, like circles.

1 Work the number of stitches up to the point where the work is to be turned. The next stitch must be wrapped with a loop of yarn before you turn the work to avoid a gap. To wrap a stitch slip the next stitch from the left-hand needle to the right-hand needle purlwise.

2 Bring the yarn forward between the needles. Carefully slip the stitch on the right-hand needle back onto the left-hand needle.

3 Yarn back. Turn the work, keeping the stitches as tight on the needle as possible at this point to ensure that the knitting is even, and work to the end of the row.

4 There will be a small bar across the wrapped stitch. These bars can be picked up and knitted together with the stitch on the final row, or the bars can be left as a feature of the shaping.

BUTTONHOLES

To create a firm and neat buttonhole, work as follows.

1 Bind (cast) off the number of stitches in pattern that are required for the buttonholes. Work to the end of the row.

2 On the next row, when you get to where you bind (cast) off stitches on the previous row, turn the work so that the other side is facing you. Cast on the same number of stitches that you cast off using the cable method (put needle between first and second stitch on left-hand needle, wrap yarn around needle and bring new loop through).

 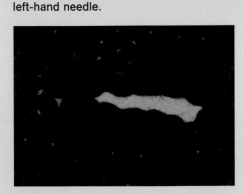

3 Before you put the last loop on the left-hand needle, bring the yarn forward between the needles. Now put the last loop onto the left-hand needle.

4 Turn the work around again, and continue until the next buttonhole. Repeat until all stitches are cast back on.

Make sure that you pull the yarn firmly and knit the stitches tightly to avoid any gaps in the work.

BINDING (CASTING) OFF SEAMS USING THREE NEEDLES

A neat, flat seam can be created by binding (casting) off stitches together. At the top of your knitted panels leave the stitches on separate stitch holders or spare needles instead of binding (casting) them off. When you are ready to join the panels, put the stitches back onto separate needles with RS facing together, making sure that both needles are pointing in the same direction. Using a third needle (that is preferably one size bigger to avoid any tightness in the seam) bind (cast) the stitches off together as follows.

1 Put the third needle into the first stitch on the first needle and the first stitch on the second needle at the same time. Wrap the yarn around the needle and bring the new loop through. Drop the first stitches off both needles that are held in your left hand.

2 Put the third needle into the next stitch on both needles and knit them together as before.

3 You will now have two stitches on the third needle. Lift the first stitch on this needle off over the second stitch. Repeat this process until all stitches have been bound (cast) off together.

BINDING (CASTING) OFF BUTTONHOLE BANDS AND BUTTONBANDS

Bands can be knitted in rather than stitched into place, enabling you to match up stitches perfectly. When you have completed the band, keep the stitches on the needle. The pattern instructions will have asked you to finish with the WS of the work facing. Using a smaller needle, pick up all of the stitches across the WS of the knitting at the beginning of the band, working from right to left. When the stitches are picked up the knitting needle should be parallel with the needle that is holding the stitches from the band. Using a third needle bind (cast) off the stitches together (see instructions for binding (casting) off seams using three needles, above).

ADDING EMBROIDERY TO KNITTING

Outlines, single dots or fancy shapes and textures can be added to your fabric after knitting. It is advisable to finish your knitting and tidy up the loose ends before embroidering. A large, blunt darning needle should be used to avoid splitting the stitches. A yarn of the same or a slightly heavier weight as the main knitting that will easily cover the stitches is recommended.

I have used Swiss darning in various projects in this book. This is a method of duplicating knitted stitches on stockinette (stocking) stitch fabrics using a needle and a separate length of yarn. It is a quick and easy way of adding dashes of color or outlines, and it can be worked horizontally or vertically.

Swiss-darning (worked horizontally)

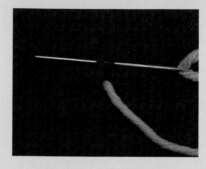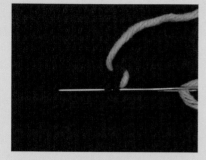

1 From the back of the work, insert the needle through the base of the knitted stitch, then take the needle around the top of the knitted stitch.

2 From the front of the work, insert the needle into the base of the same knitted stitch and out through the base of the next knitted stitch on the left.

Swiss-darning (worked vertically)

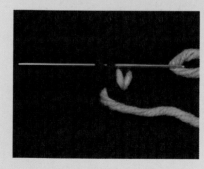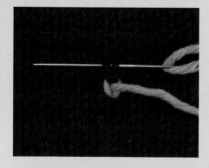

3 Pull the yarn through. You have now covered a stitch. Repeat the process until you have completed the work.

1 Darn the first stitch as for horizontal darning, but bring the needle out through the base of the stitch above the one just worked. Work that stitch in the same way. Continue forming the stitches, but work upwards rather than from right to left.

BLOCKING AND PRESSING

The blocking and pressing of knitting is an essential part of the finishing process, and one that is often omitted by knitters. There are several reasons why blocking and pressing should be done. Firstly, it flattens the edges of the knitting, which makes it easier to pick up stitches or sew together panels. Secondly, it ensures that the panels are the correct size. And lastly, it finishes the knitted fabric, and in most cases changes the physical quality of the knitting, smoothing out stitches and making the fabric feel softer and more fluid.

Blocking is the pinning out of the knitted pieces, which should be done on a flat surface with the wrong side facing up. A tape measure should be used to ensure that the pieces are of the correct size. The temperature of the iron used for pressing is dependant on the fiber content of the yarn, as is the damp or dry pressing cloth, which must completely cover the panel that is going to be pressed. The general rule is as follows: natural fibers require a damp pressing cloth and a warm iron, and synthetic fibers and mixes require a dry pressing cloth and a cool iron. However, not all yarns conform to these rules and some have alternative requirements, so it is always advisable to read the pressing instructions that are printed on the ball band. If several different yarns have been used in one piece of knitting, it is better to play safe and follow the instructions for the most delicate yarn. If the heat of the iron is too hot, it could ruin the knitting permanently, resulting in a limp and lifeless piece of knitting that is irreversible.

After pressing it is best to leave the knitting pinned out for at least half an hour to allow all of the heat and moisture to evaporate. Then, when the pins are removed, the knitting will be flat and ready for sewing up.

HOW TO FIT A ZIP

Sew in the zip before sewing together any seams. It is far easier to sew in a zip while the work is flat. With RS facing carefully tack the zip into position between the seams as indicated by the pattern instructions. Leave the ends of the work free for now. Using a strong cotton that matches the knitting, sew the zip into place using a small neat running stitch. Undo the tacking thread. Sew the seams together at either end of the zip using a neat running stitch, and making sure that the seam sits on the outside of the work. This looks much neater than the seam sitting inside, and it allows the fabric to lay flatter.

If care is taken to match the color of the zip and thread to the knitting, the zip fastening will be very discreet.

SEWING UP

After spending time knitting your cushion it is very important that the sewing together of the panels is done as neatly as possible. I would recommend that you use mattress stitch, because it is easy to learn, very precise and it creates an almost invisible seam. One big advantage of using this stitch over other methods of sewing up is that you work with the right sides of the knitting facing up towards you, which enables you to see exactly how the seam is progressing. Mattress stitch also allows you to accurately match stripes or pattern on the back and front panels of the cushion.

A blunt sewing-up needle and a matching yarn should be used to sew together the panels. Lay the pieces of knitting out on a flat surface in the arrangement in which they are to be sewn together.

Mattress stitch seam (sewing stitches to stitches)

1 From the back of the work, insert the needle through the center of the first stitch along one of the edges, leaving a long tail of yarn.

2 From the back of the work, insert the needle between the first and the second stitches along the opposite edge.

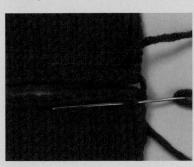

3 Continue in this way, zigzagging backwards and forwards from edge to edge, and pulling the stitches up to close the seam. Do not pull too hard or the seam will be too tight.

The mattress seam is invisible on the right side. Continue sewing the whole seam, then secure the ends by darning them in.

Mattress stitch seam (sewing rows to rows)

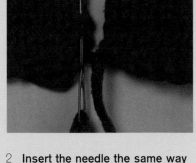

1 From the front, insert the needle between the first and second stitches on the first row. Take the needle under the next row and bring it through to the front again. Pull the yarn through, leaving a long end.

2 Insert the needle the same way into the other edge that is to be joined, but this time bring the needle out two rows above the point where it goes in.

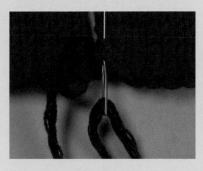

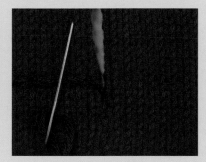

3 Insert the needle into the first edge again, into the hole that the thread last came out from on that edge. Bring the needle out two rows above that point.

4 Repeat, zigzagging from edge to edge for 2in (5cm). Pull the thread up, holding the seam and long end of the yarn with the left hand.

WASHING AND CARING FOR YOUR CUSHION

Hand-washing

Your cushion should be hand-washed to maintain its quality. Use plenty of lukewarm water and a detergent specially formulated for knitwear. The fabric should be gently squeezed and then rinsed in several changes of water. It is a good idea to get rid of excess water by gently spinning the cushion in a washing-machine inside a secure wash-bag, such as a pillowcase, to avoid the fabric stretching. This will also protect any beads or buttons. Lay the cushion out flat on a towel after washing, and gently ease back into shape. It should then be left alone until it is completely dry.

Dry-cleaning

You can have your cushion dry-cleaned, but check on all of the ball bands of the yarns that they can be dry-cleaned. Remember that if beads or buttons have been used, the dry-cleaners may refuse to clean it.

yarn information

CHOOSING THE RIGHT YARN

If you want your knitted cushion to look like the picture in the book, I would recommend that you use the yarns that I have specified for each design. A substitute yarn that differs in weight, shade or fiber content will change the whole look, feel and size of the finished piece of knitting.

QUANTITIES OF YARN AND DYE LOTS

At the beginning of each project the quantities of yarn are given for the cushion. If different yarns are used, these quantities will alter. This is because the length of a ball of yarn depends on its weight and fiber content: an aran weight cotton will have a shorter length than an aran weight wool, and a 4-ply cotton will have a longer length than a double-knit cotton. The quantities of yarn can be re-calculated if desired. Buy all the yarn you need to complete the project at the same time, checking the ball bands to ensure that all the balls are from the same dye lot. The color of a specific shade of yarn can vary quite a lot between dye lots and the change will show in the finished project.

GAUGE (TENSION) AND SELECTING CORRECT NEEDLE SIZE

The needle sizes that I have recommended for each design have been chosen to create a firm gauge (tension). This is especially important if you are knitting accessories that are going to be handled, such as cushions. If the knitting is too loose the article will easily become misshapen, and will most likely drop and grow in size. Using a slightly smaller needle than the usual recommended size for the yarn ensures that the knitted fabric retains its shape.

Gauge (tension) can differ quite dramatically between knitters. This is because of the way that the needles and the yarn are held. So if your gauge (tension) does not match that stated in the pattern you should change your needle size following this simple rule. If your knitting is too loose your gauge (tension) will read that you have less stitches and rows than the given gauge (tension), and you will need to change to a thinner needle to make the stitch size smaller. Alternatively, if your knitting is too tight your gauge (tension) will read that you have more stitches and rows than the given gauge (tension), and you will need to change to a thicker needle to make the stitch size bigger.

It should be noted that if the projects in this book are not knitted to the correct gauge (tension), yarn quantities will be effected.

YARN USED IN THIS BOOK

A selection of yarns from the Rowan Yarn collection have been used to knit all of the designs in this book. Below is a guide to the yarns that I have used, specifying their weight, length and fiber content.

Kidsilk Haze
Very lightweight mohair yarn
70% super kid mohair/ 30% silk
Approximately 230yd (210m) per
1 oz (25g) ball

Magpie Aran
Aran-weight wool yarn
100% wool
Approximately 153yd (140m) per
3½oz (100g) hank

Cork
Chunky-weight wool and nylon yarn
95% merino wool/5% nylon
Approximately 120yd (110m) per
1¾oz (50g) ball

4-ply Cotton
Very lightweight cotton yarn
100% cotton
Approximately 185yd (170m) per
1¾oz (50g) ball

Cotton Glace
Lightweight cotton yarn
100% cotton
Approximately 125yd (115m) per
1¾oz (50g) ball

Handknit DK Cotton
Medium-weight cotton yarn
100% cotton
Approximately 92yd (85m) per
1¾oz (50g) ball

Rowan Denim
Medium-weight cotton yarn
100% cotton
Approximately 101yd (93m) per
1¾oz (50g) ball

Wool Cotton
Double-knitting-weight wool and cotton
50% merino wool/ 50% cotton
Approximately 123yd (113m) per
1¾oz (50g) ball

Calmer
Medium-weight and slightly stretchy cotton and microfiber yarn
75% cotton/25% microfiber
Approximately 175yd (160m) per
1¾oz (50g) ball

All Seasons Cotton
Aran-weight cotton and microfiber yarn
60% cotton/ 40% microfiber
Approximately 98yd (90m) per
1¾oz (50g) ball

CONVERSIONS
Needle sizes

US SIZE	METRIC SIZE	OLD UK & CANADIAN SIZE
15	10	000
13	9	00
11	8	0
11	7½	1
10½	7	2
10½	6½	3
10	6	4
9	5½	5
8	5	6
7	4½	7
6	4	8
5	3¾	9
4	3½	–
3	3¼	10
2/3	3	11
2	2¾	12
1	2¼	13
0	2	14

Weights and lengths

oz	=	g × 0.0352
g	=	oz × 28.35
in	=	cm × 0.3937
cm	=	in × 2.54
yd	=	m × 0.9144
m	=	yd × 1.0936

ABBREVIATIONS

beg	beginning/begin
col	color/colorway
cont	continue
cm	centimeter
c8b	cable 8 back: slip next 4 sts onto cable needle and hold at back of work, K4, then K4 sts from the cable needle.
c10b	cable 10 back: slip next 5 sts onto cable needle and hold at back of work, [K1, P1] twice, K1, then K1, [P1, K1] twice from cable needle.
c14b	cable 14 back: slip next 7 sts onto cable needle and hold at back of work, [K1, P1] three times, K1, then work the stitches on the cable needle as folls: [K1, P1] three times, K1.
dec	decrease
dp	double pointed
foll	following
folls	follows
g	grams
in	inch
inc	increase
K	knit
k2tog	knit 2 stitches together.
mb	make bobble: knit into front, back, front, back, front, back of next stitch, [turn work (WS facing), P6, turn work again (RS facing), K6] twice, slip 2nd, 3rd, 4th, 5th and 6th sts off over 1st st, pull firmly on yarn to tighten bobble.
ml	make loop: K next st leaving st on left needle, bring yarn forward between needles, slide a bead up so that it is sitting about ¾in (2cm) away from the needle, and wrap the yarn with bead round thumb of left- hand to make a loop, take yarn between needles to back of work and K same st again, slipping st off left needle. Bring yarn forward between needles and back over needle to WS of work. Lift the 2 sts just made over this loop
mm	millimeter
m1	make one stitch.
oz	ounces
P	purl
patt	pattern
pb	place bead: thread beads onto yarn before starting to knit each section: with yarn on RS of the work, slide bead up yarn, slip 1 stitch purlwise, if necessary bring the yarn between the needles to work the next stitch.
psso	pass slipped stitch over.
p2tog	purl 2 stitches together.
rep	repeat
reps	repeats
RS	right side of work
sl	slip
st/sts	stitch/stitches
WS	wrong side of work.
yb	yarn back
yf	yarn forward
yfon	yarn forward and over needle to make a stitch.
*	repeat instructions between * as many times as instructed.
[ ]	repeat instructions between [ ] as many times as instructed.

ACKNOWLEDGMENTS

I would like to thank the following people who helped me put this book together: Lucinda Symons and Matthew Dickens for their beautiful photographs; Kate Haxell for her editorial expertise; Luise Roberts for all her hard work, constant support and encouragement; Marie Clayton at Collins and Brown; Rowan Yarns for their huge generosity again; Kate Buller for supporting me and promoting the book; Julie and Steve Cox for their invaluable advice; Marilyn Wilson for her careful pattern checking; my group of wonderful knitters who worked under extreme pressure to get the designs ready—Heddy Abrahams, Jenny Still, Ann Yockney, Michele Cooper, Liz Jenks, Julie Cox, Eleanor Yates, Hannah Brown, Caroline Norman, Helen Hadley and Helen McCarthy, and my dad who willingly transported both me and my cushions huge distances to meetings and photo-shoots at a moment's notice!

SUPPLIERS
Suppliers of Rowan Yarns and Jaeger Handknits

UK
Rowan Yarns and Jaeger Handknits
Green Lane Mill
Holmfirth
West Yorkshire
HD9 2DX
Tel: 01484 681881
www.knitrowan.com

USA
Westminster Fibers
165 Ledge Street
Nashua, NH 03031
Tel: 603 886 5041/5043

Canada
Diamond Yarn
9697 St Laurent
Montreal
Quebec H3L 2N1
Tel: 514 388 6188

155 Martin Ross
Unit 3
Toronto
Ontario M3J 2L9
Tel: 416 736 6111
www.diamondyarn.com

Australia
Australian Country Spinners
314 Albert Street
Brunswick
Victoria 3056
Tel: (03) 9380 3888

Suppliers of beads

UK
Beadworks (mail order)
16 Redbridge Enterprise Centre
Thompson Close
Ilford
Essex
IG1 1TY
Tel: 020 8553 3240
www.beadworks.co.uk

The Bead Shop
21a Tower Street
Covent Garden
London
WC2H 9NS
Tel: 020 7240 0931
www.beadshop.co.uk

Creative Beadcraft Ltd (mail order)
Unit 2
Asheridge Business Centre
Asheridge Road
Chesham
Buckinghamshire HP5 2PT
Tel: 01494 778818

20 Beak Street
London
W1F 9RE
Tel: 0207 629 9964
www.creativebeadcraft.co.uk

Mill Hill Beads
www.millhillbeads.com

USA
Global Beads
345 Castro Street
Mountain View, CA 94041
Tel: 650 967 7556
www.globalbeads.com

Keep Me In Stitches
77 Smithtown Boulevard
Smithtown, NY 11787
Tel: 631 724 8111
www.keepmeinstitches1.com

Suppliers of buttons
The ceramic buttons (that are named in the pattern instructions) are available from:

Debbie Abrahams
30 Bannerman Road
Nottingham
NG6 9HZ
Tel: 0115 9161524
www.da-handknits.demon.co.uk

All others are from Rowan Yarns and Jaeger Handknits (see contact details under yarn suppliers)

Love crafts? Crafters, keep updated on all exciting news from Collins & Brown. Email **lovecrafts@anovabooks.com** to register for **free** email alerts and author events.